50 Florida State Recipes for Home

By: Kelly Johnson

Table of Contents

- Key Lime Pie
- Cuban Sandwich
- Conch Fritters
- Gator Tail
- Florida Shrimp and Grits
- Stone Crab Claws
- Florida Orange Chicken
- Mahi-Mahi Tacos
- Cuban Black Beans and Rice
- Florida Seafood Chowder
- Hush Puppies
- Florida Style BBQ Ribs
- Southern Collard Greens
- Chicken and Sausage Gumbo
- Mojo Pork
- Florida Fruit Salad
- Jerk Chicken
- Corn and Crab Chowder
- Bahamian Conch Salad
- Plantain Chips
- Citrus-Marinated Grilled Fish
- Cuban Arroz con Pollo
- Florida Key Lime Cheesecake
- Spicy Florida Prawns
- Key West Lime Marinade
- Cuban Ropa Vieja
- Grilled Shrimp Skewers
- Florida Mango Salsa
- Southern Fried Catfish
- Florida Citrus Salad
- Mojo Chicken Wings
- Gator Gumbo
- Blackened Red Snapper
- Florida Style Fried Chicken
- Pineapple Coconut Cake
- Bahamian Johnny Cake

- Florida-Style BBQ Shrimp
- Sweet Plantain Casserole
- Caribbean Jerk Pork
- Florida Key Lime Bars
- Florida Fried Green Tomatoes
- Cuban Pork Roast
- Southern Pecan Pie
- Key West Fish Tacos
- Florida Avocado Salad
- Spicy Conch Fritters
- Florida Lime Chicken
- Cuban Beef Empanadas
- Tropical Fruit Smoothie
- Florida Peach Cobbler

Key Lime Pie

Ingredients:

For the Crust:

- 1 ½ cups graham cracker crumbs
- ⅓ cup granulated sugar
- 6 tablespoons unsalted butter, melted

For the Filling:

- 4 large egg yolks
- 1 can (14 ounces) sweetened condensed milk
- ½ cup fresh key lime juice (or regular lime juice if key limes are unavailable)
- 1 tablespoon grated lime zest

For the Topping:

- 1 cup heavy cream
- 2 tablespoons granulated sugar
- Lime slices or wedges for garnish (optional)

Instructions:

1. **Preheat the Oven:** Preheat your oven to 350°F (175°C).
2. **Prepare the Crust:**
   - In a medium bowl, combine graham cracker crumbs, sugar, and melted butter. Mix until well combined.
   - Press the mixture evenly into the bottom and up the sides of a 9-inch pie dish.
   - Bake for 8-10 minutes, or until the crust is lightly golden. Allow to cool.
3. **Make the Filling:**
   - In a large bowl, whisk together egg yolks until smooth.
   - Gradually mix in sweetened condensed milk until well combined.
   - Stir in the lime juice and lime zest until fully incorporated.
   - Pour the filling into the cooled crust.
4. **Bake the Pie:**
   - Bake in the preheated oven for 15-18 minutes, or until the filling is set and the surface is slightly puffed. The center should still jiggle slightly.
   - Remove from the oven and let cool to room temperature. Refrigerate for at least 4 hours, or until thoroughly chilled.
5. **Prepare the Topping:**
   - In a medium bowl, beat heavy cream with granulated sugar until stiff peaks form.
   - Spread or pipe the whipped cream over the chilled pie.
6. **Garnish and Serve:**

- Garnish with lime slices or wedges, if desired.
- Slice and serve chilled.

Enjoy your homemade Key Lime Pie!

Cuban Sandwich

Ingredients:

For the Sandwich:

- 1 loaf Cuban bread (or Italian bread if Cuban is unavailable)
- 2 tablespoons yellow mustard
- 4 ounces sliced roast pork (cooked and seasoned)
- 4 ounces sliced ham
- 4 ounces Swiss cheese
- 4-6 dill pickle slices (or more to taste)
- 2 tablespoons butter (for grilling)

Instructions:

1. **Preheat Your Press:**
   - Preheat a panini press or a grill pan over medium heat.
2. **Prepare the Bread:**
   - Slice the Cuban bread lengthwise. If using Italian bread, slice it into a similar shape.
3. **Assemble the Sandwich:**
   - Spread mustard evenly on the inside of both halves of the bread.
   - On the bottom half of the bread, layer the roast pork, ham, Swiss cheese, and pickle slices.
   - Top with the other half of the bread.
4. **Grill the Sandwich:**
   - Butter the outside of both halves of the sandwich.
   - Place the sandwich in the preheated panini press or grill pan.
   - If using a grill pan, press down with a heavy skillet or another pan to flatten the sandwich. Cook for about 4-6 minutes, or until the bread is crispy and golden brown and the cheese is melted.
   - If using a panini press, follow the manufacturer's instructions for grilling time.
5. **Serve:**
   - Remove the sandwich from the heat and let it rest for a minute before slicing.
   - Cut the sandwich into halves or quarters and serve warm.

Enjoy your authentic Cuban Sandwich!

Conch Fritters

Ingredients:

For the Fritters:

- 1 pound conch meat (fresh or frozen, finely chopped)
- 1 cup all-purpose flour
- 1 teaspoon baking powder
- ½ teaspoon baking soda
- ½ teaspoon salt
- ¼ teaspoon black pepper
- ¼ teaspoon cayenne pepper (optional, for heat)
- 1 teaspoon paprika
- ½ cup finely chopped onion
- ½ cup finely chopped bell pepper (red or green)
- 2 cloves garlic, minced
- 2 large eggs
- ¾ cup buttermilk (or regular milk if unavailable)
- 2 tablespoons chopped fresh parsley (optional)
- Vegetable oil, for frying

For the Dipping Sauce (optional):

- ½ cup mayonnaise
- 2 tablespoons ketchup
- 1 tablespoon lime juice
- 1 teaspoon hot sauce (optional)

Instructions:

1. **Prepare the Fritter Batter:**
   - In a large bowl, whisk together flour, baking powder, baking soda, salt, black pepper, cayenne pepper (if using), and paprika.
   - Stir in the chopped conch meat, onion, bell pepper, garlic, and parsley (if using).
   - In a separate bowl, beat the eggs and mix with the buttermilk.
   - Pour the egg mixture into the dry ingredients and stir until just combined. The batter should be thick but spoonable.
2. **Heat the Oil:**
   - In a large skillet or deep fryer, heat about 2 inches of vegetable oil to 350°F (175°C). You can test if the oil is ready by dropping a small bit of batter into it; it should sizzle and float to the surface.
3. **Fry the Fritters:**
   - Drop spoonfuls of the batter into the hot oil, being careful not to overcrowd the pan. Fry in batches if necessary.

- Cook for about 2-3 minutes per side, or until the fritters are golden brown and crispy.
- Use a slotted spoon to transfer the fritters to a paper towel-lined plate to drain excess oil.

4. **Prepare the Dipping Sauce (if using):**
   - In a small bowl, mix together mayonnaise, ketchup, lime juice, and hot sauce (if using). Adjust seasoning to taste.

5. **Serve:**
   - Serve the conch fritters warm with the dipping sauce on the side.

Enjoy your Conch Fritters!

Gator Tail

Ingredients:

For the Gator Tail:

- 1 pound gator tail meat, cut into bite-sized pieces
- 1 cup buttermilk
- 1 cup all-purpose flour
- 1 cup cornmeal
- 1 tablespoon paprika
- 1 teaspoon garlic powder
- 1 teaspoon onion powder
- 1 teaspoon cayenne pepper (optional, for heat)
- 1 teaspoon salt
- ½ teaspoon black pepper
- Vegetable oil, for frying

For the Dipping Sauce (optional):

- ½ cup mayonnaise
- 2 tablespoons hot sauce (adjust to taste)
- 1 tablespoon lemon juice
- 1 teaspoon garlic powder

Instructions:

1. **Marinate the Gator Tail:**
   - Place the gator tail pieces in a bowl and pour buttermilk over them. Cover and refrigerate for at least 1 hour (or up to overnight) to marinate.
2. **Prepare the Breading:**
   - In a large bowl, combine flour, cornmeal, paprika, garlic powder, onion powder, cayenne pepper (if using), salt, and black pepper. Mix well.
3. **Heat the Oil:**
   - In a large skillet or deep fryer, heat about 2 inches of vegetable oil to 350°F (175°C).
4. **Bread the Gator Tail:**
   - Remove the gator tail pieces from the buttermilk, allowing any excess to drip off.
   - Dredge the pieces in the flour mixture, coating them evenly. Shake off any excess flour mixture.
5. **Fry the Gator Tail:**
   - Carefully add the breaded gator tail pieces to the hot oil, working in batches if necessary to avoid overcrowding.
   - Fry for about 4-5 minutes, or until the pieces are golden brown and crispy, and the internal temperature reaches 165°F (74°C).

- Use a slotted spoon to transfer the gator tail pieces to a paper towel-lined plate to drain excess oil.
6. **Prepare the Dipping Sauce (if using):**
    - In a small bowl, mix together mayonnaise, hot sauce, lemon juice, and garlic powder. Adjust seasoning to taste.
7. **Serve:**
    - Serve the fried gator tail warm with the dipping sauce on the side.

Enjoy your crispy and flavorful Gator Tail!

Florida Shrimp and Grits

Ingredients:

For the Shrimp:

- 1 pound large shrimp, peeled and deveined
- 2 tablespoons olive oil
- 4 cloves garlic, minced
- 1 teaspoon smoked paprika
- 1 teaspoon Old Bay seasoning
- ½ teaspoon cayenne pepper (optional, for heat)
- Salt and black pepper to taste
- 1 tablespoon lemon juice
- 2 tablespoons chopped fresh parsley (for garnish)

For the Grits:

- 1 cup stone-ground grits
- 4 cups water or chicken broth
- 1 cup shredded sharp cheddar cheese
- 2 tablespoons unsalted butter
- ½ cup heavy cream
- Salt and black pepper to taste

Instructions:

1. **Prepare the Grits:**
    - In a medium saucepan, bring water or chicken broth to a boil.
    - Slowly whisk in the grits, reducing heat to low. Cover and simmer, stirring occasionally, for about 20-25 minutes, or until the grits are tender and creamy.
    - Once cooked, stir in the shredded cheddar cheese, butter, and heavy cream. Season with salt and black pepper to taste. Keep warm.
2. **Cook the Shrimp:**
    - In a large skillet, heat olive oil over medium-high heat.
    - Add minced garlic and cook for about 1 minute, or until fragrant.
    - Add the shrimp to the skillet and season with smoked paprika, Old Bay seasoning, cayenne pepper (if using), salt, and black pepper.
    - Cook for 2-3 minutes per side, or until the shrimp are pink and opaque. Be careful not to overcook.
    - Stir in the lemon juice and cook for an additional 1 minute. Remove from heat.
3. **Serve:**
    - Spoon the creamy grits onto serving plates.
    - Top with the seasoned shrimp.
    - Garnish with chopped fresh parsley.

Enjoy your delicious Florida Shrimp and Grits!

Stone Crab Claws

Ingredients:

For the Stone Crab Claws:

- 1 pound stone crab claws (pre-cooked or raw, if cooking yourself)
- 1 lemon, cut into wedges
- 1-2 tablespoons Old Bay seasoning or crab boil seasoning (optional)
- 4 cups water (for boiling, if raw)

For the Mustard Sauce:

- ¼ cup mayonnaise
- 2 tablespoons Dijon mustard
- 1 tablespoon yellow mustard
- 1 tablespoon lemon juice
- 1 teaspoon hot sauce (optional)
- Salt and black pepper to taste

Instructions:

1. **Prepare the Claws:**
   - If you have raw stone crab claws, bring 4 cups of water to a boil in a large pot. Add Old Bay seasoning or crab boil seasoning if desired.
   - Carefully add the claws to the boiling water. Boil for about 10-15 minutes, or until the claws turn bright orange and are cooked through.
   - Remove the claws from the pot and place them in an ice bath or under cold running water to stop the cooking process. Drain and let cool.
2. **Serve the Claws:**
   - If using pre-cooked claws, simply thaw them if frozen, and rinse under cold water to remove any ice crystals.
   - Serve the claws cold or at room temperature with lemon wedges.
3. **Prepare the Mustard Sauce:**
   - In a small bowl, combine mayonnaise, Dijon mustard, yellow mustard, lemon juice, and hot sauce (if using).
   - Mix well and season with salt and black pepper to taste.
4. **Serve:**
   - Arrange the stone crab claws on a platter.
   - Serve with the mustard sauce and lemon wedges on the side.

Enjoy your delicious Stone Crab Claws!

Florida Orange Chicken

Ingredients:

For the Chicken:

- 1 pound boneless, skinless chicken breasts or thighs, cut into bite-sized pieces
- 1 cup all-purpose flour
- 1 teaspoon salt
- ½ teaspoon black pepper
- ½ teaspoon garlic powder
- ½ teaspoon onion powder
- 2 large eggs, beaten
- Vegetable oil, for frying

For the Orange Sauce:

- 1 cup orange juice (freshly squeezed or store-bought)
- ¼ cup soy sauce
- ¼ cup rice vinegar
- ¼ cup brown sugar
- 2 tablespoons cornstarch mixed with 2 tablespoons water (for thickening)
- 1 tablespoon grated fresh ginger
- 2 cloves garlic, minced
- 1 teaspoon sesame oil
- 1 teaspoon red pepper flakes (optional, for heat)

For Garnish:

- 2 green onions, sliced
- Sesame seeds (optional)

Instructions:

1. **Prepare the Chicken:**
   - In a shallow bowl, combine flour, salt, black pepper, garlic powder, and onion powder.
   - Dredge the chicken pieces in the flour mixture, shaking off any excess.
   - Dip the floured chicken pieces into the beaten eggs, then coat again with the flour mixture.
2. **Fry the Chicken:**
   - Heat about 2 inches of vegetable oil in a large skillet or deep fryer over medium-high heat.
   - Fry the chicken in batches until golden brown and cooked through, about 4-5 minutes per batch.

- Use a slotted spoon to transfer the chicken to a paper towel-lined plate to drain.
3. **Prepare the Orange Sauce:**
    - In a medium saucepan, combine orange juice, soy sauce, rice vinegar, brown sugar, grated ginger, minced garlic, sesame oil, and red pepper flakes (if using).
    - Bring the mixture to a boil over medium heat, stirring occasionally.
    - Reduce heat and simmer for about 2 minutes.
    - Stir in the cornstarch mixture and continue to simmer until the sauce thickens, about 1-2 minutes. Remove from heat.
4. **Combine Chicken and Sauce:**
    - In a large bowl or serving dish, toss the fried chicken pieces with the orange sauce until evenly coated.
5. **Serve:**
    - Garnish with sliced green onions and sesame seeds, if desired.
    - Serve the Florida Orange Chicken over steamed rice or with vegetables.

Enjoy your tangy and flavorful Florida Orange Chicken!

Mahi-Mahi Tacos

Ingredients:

For the Mahi-Mahi:

- 1 pound mahi-mahi fillets, skinless
- 2 tablespoons olive oil
- 1 teaspoon ground cumin
- 1 teaspoon smoked paprika
- 1 teaspoon garlic powder
- ½ teaspoon onion powder
- ½ teaspoon chili powder
- ½ teaspoon salt
- ¼ teaspoon black pepper
- Juice of 1 lime

For the Slaw:

- 2 cups shredded cabbage (green or purple, or a mix)
- 1 medium carrot, grated
- ¼ cup chopped fresh cilantro
- 2 tablespoons lime juice
- 2 tablespoons mayonnaise
- 1 tablespoon honey
- Salt and pepper to taste

For the Tacos:

- 8 small corn or flour tortillas
- ½ avocado, sliced (optional)
- 1 jalapeño, thinly sliced (optional)
- Lime wedges (for serving)

Instructions:

1. **Prepare the Mahi-Mahi:**
   - Preheat your grill or a large skillet over medium-high heat.
   - In a small bowl, mix together the ground cumin, smoked paprika, garlic powder, onion powder, chili powder, salt, and black pepper.
   - Rub the mahi-mahi fillets with olive oil and then coat them with the spice mixture.
   - Grill or pan-sear the mahi-mahi for about 3-4 minutes per side, or until the fish is opaque and flakes easily with a fork. Squeeze lime juice over the fish after cooking.
2. **Make the Slaw:**

    - In a large bowl, combine shredded cabbage, grated carrot, and chopped cilantro.
    - In a small bowl, whisk together lime juice, mayonnaise, and honey.
    - Pour the dressing over the slaw mixture and toss to combine. Season with salt and pepper to taste.
3. **Prepare the Tacos:**
    - Warm the tortillas in a dry skillet or directly over a flame until they are pliable and lightly charred.
    - Flake the cooked mahi-mahi into bite-sized pieces.
4. **Assemble the Tacos:**
    - Place a few pieces of mahi-mahi in the center of each tortilla.
    - Top with a generous amount of slaw.
    - Add avocado slices and jalapeño slices, if desired.
5. **Serve:**
    - Serve the tacos with lime wedges on the side for extra zing.

Enjoy your fresh and flavorful Mahi-Mahi Tacos!

Cuban Black Beans and Rice

Ingredients:

For the Black Beans:

- 1 pound dried black beans (or 2 cans of black beans, drained and rinsed)
- 1 bay leaf
- 1 teaspoon dried oregano
- 1 teaspoon ground cumin
- 1 onion, finely chopped
- 1 bell pepper (red or green), finely chopped
- 4 cloves garlic, minced
- 2 tablespoons olive oil
- 1 can (14.5 ounces) diced tomatoes
- 1 tablespoon tomato paste
- 1 tablespoon red wine vinegar
- Salt and black pepper to taste
- 2 cups chicken or vegetable broth (or water)

For the Rice:

- 1 cup long-grain white rice
- 2 cups water
- 1 tablespoon olive oil
- 1 teaspoon salt

For Garnish (optional):

- Chopped fresh cilantro
- Lime wedges
- Sliced avocado

Instructions:

1. **Prepare the Black Beans:**
    - **If using dried beans:** Rinse and soak the beans overnight in plenty of water. Drain and rinse before cooking.
    - In a large pot, combine the soaked beans, bay leaf, oregano, cumin, and enough water or broth to cover the beans by about 2 inches. Bring to a boil.
    - Reduce heat, cover, and simmer for about 1-1.5 hours, or until the beans are tender. Add more water or broth as needed to keep the beans covered during cooking.
    - **If using canned beans:** Skip the soaking and cooking steps. Simply add the canned beans to the pot in the following steps.

2. **Cook the Bean Seasoning:**
   - In a separate large skillet, heat olive oil over medium heat.
   - Add chopped onion and bell pepper and cook until softened, about 5 minutes.
   - Stir in minced garlic and cook for another 1-2 minutes until fragrant.
   - Add the diced tomatoes, tomato paste, and red wine vinegar. Stir to combine.
3. **Combine Beans and Seasoning:**
   - Once the beans are tender, add the onion and bell pepper mixture to the pot of beans.
   - Stir well and simmer for an additional 15-20 minutes to allow the flavors to meld. Season with salt and black pepper to taste.
4. **Prepare the Rice:**
   - In a medium saucepan, heat olive oil over medium heat.
   - Add the rice and cook, stirring frequently, until lightly toasted, about 2-3 minutes.
   - Add water and salt. Bring to a boil.
   - Reduce heat to low, cover, and simmer for about 18-20 minutes, or until the rice is tender and water is absorbed. Remove from heat and let it sit, covered, for 5 minutes before fluffing with a fork.
5. **Serve:**
   - Serve the black beans over a bed of rice.
   - Garnish with chopped fresh cilantro, lime wedges, and sliced avocado, if desired.

Enjoy your hearty and delicious Cuban Black Beans and Rice!

Florida Seafood Chowder

Ingredients:

For the Chowder:

- 2 tablespoons unsalted butter
- 1 medium onion, finely chopped
- 2 cloves garlic, minced
- 2 celery stalks, diced
- 1 medium carrot, diced
- 1 bell pepper (red or green), diced
- 1 large potato, peeled and diced
- 4 cups seafood stock (or chicken/vegetable broth)
- 1 cup heavy cream
- 1 cup whole milk
- 1 teaspoon dried thyme
- 1 teaspoon dried oregano
- 1 bay leaf
- 1 cup corn kernels (fresh, frozen, or canned)
- 1 pound mixed seafood (e.g., shrimp, scallops, clams, and/or white fish), cut into bite-sized pieces
- 1 tablespoon lemon juice
- Salt and black pepper to taste
- 2 tablespoons chopped fresh parsley (for garnish)

Instructions:

1. **Sauté the Vegetables:**
    - In a large pot, melt the butter over medium heat.
    - Add the chopped onion, garlic, celery, carrot, and bell pepper. Cook until the vegetables are softened, about 5-7 minutes.
2. **Add Potatoes and Stock:**
    - Stir in the diced potato and cook for another 2 minutes.
    - Add the seafood stock (or broth) and bay leaf. Bring to a boil, then reduce the heat and simmer until the potatoes are tender, about 10-15 minutes.
3. **Make it Creamy:**
    - Stir in the heavy cream and milk. Add dried thyme, dried oregano, and corn kernels. Continue to cook over low heat, stirring occasionally, until the mixture is heated through.
4. **Add the Seafood:**
    - Gently add the mixed seafood to the pot. Cook until the seafood is cooked through and opaque, about 4-5 minutes. Be careful not to overcook the seafood.
5. **Season and Finish:**

- Stir in the lemon juice and season with salt and black pepper to taste.
- Remove the bay leaf.
6. **Serve:**
    - Ladle the chowder into bowls and garnish with chopped fresh parsley.

Enjoy your delicious and hearty Florida Seafood Chowder!

Hush Puppies

Ingredients:

- 1 cup cornmeal
- 1 cup all-purpose flour
- 2 tablespoons granulated sugar
- 1 tablespoon baking powder
- 1 teaspoon salt
- ½ teaspoon black pepper
- ½ teaspoon cayenne pepper (optional, for heat)
- 1 small onion, finely chopped
- 1 large egg
- 1 cup buttermilk (or regular milk if unavailable)
- Vegetable oil, for frying

Instructions:

1. **Prepare the Dry Ingredients:**
    - In a large bowl, whisk together the cornmeal, flour, sugar, baking powder, salt, black pepper, and cayenne pepper (if using).
2. **Add the Wet Ingredients:**
    - Stir in the finely chopped onion.
    - In a separate bowl, whisk the egg and buttermilk together.
    - Pour the wet mixture into the dry ingredients and stir until just combined. The batter will be thick.
3. **Heat the Oil:**
    - In a large skillet or deep fryer, heat about 2 inches of vegetable oil to 350°F (175°C). You can test if the oil is hot enough by dropping a small spoonful of batter into it; it should sizzle and float to the surface.
4. **Fry the Hush Puppies:**
    - Drop spoonfuls of the batter into the hot oil, being careful not to overcrowd the pan. Fry in batches if necessary.
    - Cook for about 2-3 minutes per side, or until the hush puppies are golden brown and crispy.
    - Use a slotted spoon to transfer the hush puppies to a paper towel-lined plate to drain excess oil.
5. **Serve:**
    - Serve the hush puppies warm as a side dish or appetizer.

Enjoy your crispy and delicious Hush Puppies!

Florida Style BBQ Ribs

Ingredients:

For the Ribs:

- 2 racks of baby back ribs (about 2-3 pounds each)
- 2 tablespoons olive oil
- 1 tablespoon smoked paprika
- 1 tablespoon garlic powder
- 1 tablespoon onion powder
- 1 teaspoon ground cumin
- 1 teaspoon chili powder
- 1 teaspoon dried oregano
- 1 teaspoon salt
- ½ teaspoon black pepper

For the Florida BBQ Sauce:

- 1 cup orange juice (preferably freshly squeezed)
- ½ cup ketchup
- ¼ cup brown sugar
- ¼ cup apple cider vinegar
- 2 tablespoons soy sauce
- 1 tablespoon Dijon mustard
- 1 tablespoon Worcestershire sauce
- 1 teaspoon garlic powder
- 1 teaspoon onion powder
- ½ teaspoon smoked paprika
- ¼ teaspoon cayenne pepper (optional, for heat)
- Salt and black pepper to taste

Instructions:

1. **Prepare the Ribs:**
    - Preheat your oven to 300°F (150°C).
    - Remove the silver skin from the back of the ribs (the thin membrane) for better tenderness.
    - Rub the ribs with olive oil.
    - In a small bowl, mix together smoked paprika, garlic powder, onion powder, ground cumin, chili powder, dried oregano, salt, and black pepper.
    - Rub the spice mixture evenly over both sides of the ribs.
2. **Cook the Ribs:**
    - Place the ribs on a baking sheet lined with aluminum foil. You can also use a rack on the baking sheet if you prefer.

- Cover the ribs with another piece of aluminum foil.
- Bake in the preheated oven for 2.5-3 hours, or until the ribs are tender.

3. **Prepare the BBQ Sauce:**
    - While the ribs are baking, in a medium saucepan, combine orange juice, ketchup, brown sugar, apple cider vinegar, soy sauce, Dijon mustard, Worcestershire sauce, garlic powder, onion powder, smoked paprika, and cayenne pepper (if using).
    - Bring to a simmer over medium heat, stirring occasionally.
    - Reduce the heat and simmer for about 15-20 minutes, or until the sauce has thickened slightly.
    - Season with salt and black pepper to taste. Remove from heat.

4. **Finish the Ribs:**
    - Preheat your grill to medium-high heat.
    - Remove the ribs from the oven and discard the top layer of foil.
    - Brush a generous amount of the Florida BBQ sauce over the ribs.
    - Transfer the ribs to the grill and cook for about 5-7 minutes per side, basting with more sauce and turning occasionally, until the ribs are caramelized and slightly charred.

5. **Serve:**
    - Remove the ribs from the grill and let them rest for a few minutes before cutting.
    - Serve with extra BBQ sauce on the side.

Enjoy your Florida Style BBQ Ribs with their citrusy, tangy flavors!

Southern Collard Greens

Ingredients:

- 2 pounds fresh collard greens (about 2 large bunches)
- 4 slices bacon (or 2 tablespoons bacon grease)
- 1 large onion, chopped
- 4 cloves garlic, minced
- 1 smoked ham hock (or 2 smoked turkey wings for a leaner option)
- 4 cups chicken or vegetable broth
- 1 teaspoon sugar
- 1 teaspoon apple cider vinegar
- ½ teaspoon crushed red pepper flakes (optional, for heat)
- Salt and black pepper to taste

Instructions:

1. **Prepare the Collard Greens:**
    - Rinse the collard greens thoroughly in cold water to remove any grit or dirt.
    - Remove the tough stems from the collard greens and discard them.
    - Stack the leaves, roll them up, and cut into strips about 1-inch wide.
2. **Cook the Bacon:**
    - In a large pot or Dutch oven, cook the bacon over medium heat until crispy.
    - Remove the bacon with a slotted spoon and set aside, leaving the rendered fat in the pot. If using bacon grease, add it to the pot.
3. **Sauté the Aromatics:**
    - Add the chopped onion to the pot with the bacon fat and cook until softened, about 5 minutes.
    - Add the minced garlic and cook for an additional 1-2 minutes until fragrant.
4. **Add the Ham Hock:**
    - Add the smoked ham hock to the pot. If using smoked turkey wings, add them at this point.
5. **Add the Collard Greens:**
    - Add the collard greens to the pot in batches, stirring to wilt down each batch before adding more.
    - Once all the greens are in the pot, pour in the chicken or vegetable broth.
6. **Simmer:**
    - Stir in the sugar, apple cider vinegar, and crushed red pepper flakes (if using).
    - Bring to a boil, then reduce the heat to low.
    - Cover and simmer for 45 minutes to 1 hour, or until the collard greens are tender and flavorful. Stir occasionally.
7. **Season and Serve:**
    - Remove the ham hock (or turkey wings) from the pot. Shred the meat from the bone, discard the bones, and return the meat to the pot.

- Season the collard greens with salt and black pepper to taste.
- Chop the reserved bacon and sprinkle it over the top, or mix it in.

Enjoy your Southern Collard Greens, which are perfect as a hearty side dish!

Chicken and Sausage Gumbo

Ingredients:

For the Gumbo:

- 1 pound chicken thighs, boneless and skinless, cut into bite-sized pieces
- 1 pound andouille sausage, sliced (or other smoked sausage)
- ¼ cup vegetable oil
- ¼ cup all-purpose flour
- 1 large onion, finely chopped
- 1 bell pepper (green or red), finely chopped
- 3 celery stalks, finely chopped
- 4 cloves garlic, minced
- 1 can (14.5 ounces) diced tomatoes
- 6 cups chicken broth
- 2 bay leaves
- 1 teaspoon dried thyme
- 1 teaspoon paprika
- 1 teaspoon ground cumin
- ½ teaspoon cayenne pepper (adjust to taste)
- 1 cup frozen okra (or fresh if available)
- 1 cup chopped green onions (for garnish)
- ¼ cup chopped fresh parsley (for garnish)
- Salt and black pepper to taste
- Cooked white rice (for serving)

Instructions:

1. **Brown the Meat:**
    - In a large pot or Dutch oven, heat a bit of oil over medium-high heat.
    - Add the chicken pieces and sausage. Cook until browned on all sides. Remove the meat and set aside.
2. **Make the Roux:**
    - In the same pot, add the vegetable oil and heat over medium heat.
    - Gradually whisk in the flour, creating a roux. Stir constantly to prevent burning.
    - Continue cooking and stirring until the roux turns a deep brown color (about 15-20 minutes).
3. **Cook the Vegetables:**
    - Add the chopped onion, bell pepper, and celery to the pot with the roux. Cook until softened, about 5-7 minutes.
    - Stir in the minced garlic and cook for another minute.
4. **Add Liquids and Seasonings:**
    - Stir in the diced tomatoes.

- Gradually add the chicken broth, stirring constantly to combine with the roux.
- Add the bay leaves, dried thyme, paprika, ground cumin, and cayenne pepper. Stir well.

5. **Simmer the Gumbo:**
   - Return the browned chicken and sausage to the pot.
   - Bring the gumbo to a boil, then reduce the heat to low.
   - Cover and simmer for about 45 minutes to 1 hour, or until the chicken is cooked through and tender.

6. **Add Okra:**
   - Stir in the frozen okra (or fresh okra if using). Continue to cook for another 15-20 minutes, or until the okra is tender.

7. **Adjust Seasoning:**
   - Taste and adjust seasoning with salt and black pepper as needed.
   - Remove the bay leaves.

8. **Serve:**
   - Ladle the gumbo over cooked white rice.
   - Garnish with chopped green onions and fresh parsley.

Enjoy your flavorful Chicken and Sausage Gumbo, perfect for a comforting meal!

Mojo Pork

Ingredients:

For the Mojo Marinade:

- 1 cup orange juice (freshly squeezed is best)
- ¼ cup lime juice (freshly squeezed)
- 6 cloves garlic, minced
- 1 tablespoon ground cumin
- 1 tablespoon dried oregano
- 1 teaspoon smoked paprika
- 1 teaspoon salt
- ½ teaspoon black pepper
- ¼ cup olive oil
- 1 tablespoon white vinegar
- 1 small onion, finely chopped
- 1 jalapeño or serrano pepper, minced (optional, for heat)

For the Pork:

- 2-3 pounds pork shoulder (also known as pork butt), trimmed and cut into large chunks

Instructions:

1. **Prepare the Mojo Marinade:**
   - In a bowl, whisk together orange juice, lime juice, minced garlic, ground cumin, dried oregano, smoked paprika, salt, black pepper, olive oil, white vinegar, and chopped onion. If using, add the minced jalapeño or serrano pepper for extra heat.
2. **Marinate the Pork:**
   - Place the pork shoulder chunks in a large resealable plastic bag or a shallow dish.
   - Pour the mojo marinade over the pork, making sure it's well-coated.
   - Seal the bag or cover the dish and refrigerate for at least 4 hours, preferably overnight, to allow the flavors to infuse.
3. **Cook the Pork:**
   - **For Oven Roasting:**
     - Preheat your oven to 300°F (150°C).
     - Remove the pork from the marinade (discard the marinade) and place the pork in a roasting pan.
     - Cover the pan with aluminum foil and roast for about 3-4 hours, or until the pork is tender and easily shreds with a fork.

- For a crispy exterior, remove the foil during the last 30 minutes of cooking and increase the oven temperature to 400°F (200°C). Roast until the outside is browned and crispy.
  - **For Slow Cooking:**
    - Transfer the marinated pork and any leftover marinade to a slow cooker.
    - Cover and cook on low for 6-8 hours, or until the pork is tender and shreds easily.
  - **For Grilling:**
    - Preheat your grill to medium-high heat.
    - Remove the pork from the marinade (discard the marinade) and grill, turning occasionally, until the pork is cooked through and has a nice char, about 20-30 minutes depending on the thickness of the pork. Use a meat thermometer to ensure the internal temperature reaches 145°F (63°C).

4. **Shred and Serve:**
   - Once cooked, let the pork rest for about 10 minutes before shredding it with two forks.
   - Serve the mojo pork with your favorite sides such as rice, black beans, plantains, or on sandwiches.

Enjoy your Mojo Pork, bursting with zesty and savory flavors!

Florida Fruit Salad

Ingredients:

- 2 cups fresh pineapple, diced
- 2 cups fresh strawberries, hulled and halved
- 2 cups fresh mango, diced
- 1 cup fresh blueberries
- 1 cup fresh kiwi, peeled and sliced
- 1 orange, peeled and segmented
- 1 tablespoon fresh lime juice
- 1 tablespoon honey or agave syrup (optional, for extra sweetness)
- ¼ cup chopped fresh mint (optional, for garnish)

Instructions:

1. **Prepare the Fruit:**
    - Dice the pineapple, mango, and kiwi into bite-sized pieces.
    - Hull and halve the strawberries.
    - Peel and segment the orange.
    - Wash the blueberries.
2. **Combine the Ingredients:**
    - In a large mixing bowl, combine all the prepared fruit: pineapple, strawberries, mango, blueberries, kiwi, and orange segments.
3. **Make the Dressing:**
    - In a small bowl, whisk together the fresh lime juice and honey (or agave syrup) if using.
4. **Toss the Salad:**
    - Drizzle the lime juice mixture over the fruit salad.
    - Gently toss the fruit to combine and evenly coat with the dressing.
5. **Garnish and Serve:**
    - If desired, sprinkle chopped fresh mint over the fruit salad for added flavor and garnish.
    - Serve immediately, or refrigerate for up to an hour before serving to allow the flavors to meld.

Enjoy your vibrant and refreshing Florida Fruit Salad!

Jerk Chicken

Ingredients:

For the Jerk Marinade:

- 4-6 chicken thighs or drumsticks (bone-in, skin-on for best flavor)
- 1 medium onion, chopped
- 4 cloves garlic, minced
- 2-3 Scotch bonnet peppers (or habanero peppers), seeded and chopped (adjust to taste for heat)
- 1 tablespoon fresh ginger, grated
- 2 tablespoons fresh thyme leaves (or 1 tablespoon dried thyme)
- 2 tablespoons brown sugar
- 1 tablespoon ground allspice
- 1 teaspoon ground cinnamon
- 1 teaspoon ground nutmeg
- 1 teaspoon paprika
- 1 teaspoon ground black pepper
- 1 teaspoon salt
- ¼ cup soy sauce
- ¼ cup white vinegar
- 2 tablespoons vegetable oil
- Juice of 1 lime

Instructions:

1. **Prepare the Marinade:**
   - In a food processor or blender, combine the onion, garlic, Scotch bonnet peppers, ginger, thyme, brown sugar, allspice, cinnamon, nutmeg, paprika, black pepper, salt, soy sauce, white vinegar, vegetable oil, and lime juice.
   - Blend until you have a smooth paste.
2. **Marinate the Chicken:**
   - Place the chicken pieces in a large resealable plastic bag or a shallow dish.
   - Pour the jerk marinade over the chicken, making sure all pieces are well coated.
   - Seal the bag or cover the dish and refrigerate for at least 2 hours, preferably overnight, to allow the flavors to penetrate the chicken.
3. **Grill the Chicken:**
   - Preheat your grill to medium-high heat.
   - Remove the chicken from the marinade and let any excess drip off.
   - Grill the chicken, turning occasionally, until the internal temperature reaches 165°F (74°C) and the skin is crispy and charred in spots, about 25-30 minutes.
4. **Alternative Cooking Methods:**

- **Oven:** Preheat your oven to 375°F (190°C). Place the marinated chicken on a baking sheet and bake for 35-40 minutes, or until the chicken reaches an internal temperature of 165°F (74°C) and the skin is crispy.
    - **Broiler:** Preheat the broiler. Place the chicken on a broiler pan and broil for 20-25 minutes, turning once, until the chicken is cooked through and has a nice char.
5. **Rest and Serve:**
    - Let the chicken rest for a few minutes before serving.
    - Serve with traditional sides like rice and peas, fried plantains, or a fresh salad.

Enjoy your spicy and aromatic Jerk Chicken, perfect for a taste of the Caribbean!

Corn and Crab Chowder

Ingredients:

- 1 pound fresh or frozen crab meat (or 1 can of crab meat, drained)
- 4 slices bacon, diced
- 1 medium onion, finely chopped
- 2 cloves garlic, minced
- 2 celery stalks, diced
- 1 large carrot, diced
- 4 cups fresh or frozen corn kernels (about 4-5 ears of corn, or 2 cans, drained)
- 4 cups chicken or vegetable broth
- 1 cup heavy cream
- 1 cup whole milk
- 2 large potatoes, peeled and diced
- 1 teaspoon dried thyme
- 1 bay leaf
- 1 tablespoon fresh lemon juice
- Salt and black pepper to taste
- 2 tablespoons chopped fresh parsley (for garnish)
- 2 tablespoons all-purpose flour (optional, for thickening)

Instructions:

1. **Cook the Bacon:**
    - In a large pot or Dutch oven, cook the diced bacon over medium heat until crispy.
    - Remove the bacon with a slotted spoon and set aside, leaving the rendered fat in the pot.
2. **Sauté the Vegetables:**
    - Add the chopped onion, garlic, celery, and carrot to the pot. Cook until the vegetables are softened, about 5-7 minutes.
3. **Add Corn and Potatoes:**
    - Stir in the corn kernels and diced potatoes. Cook for an additional 2-3 minutes.
4. **Add Broth and Seasonings:**
    - Pour in the chicken or vegetable broth.
    - Stir in the dried thyme and bay leaf.
    - Bring to a boil, then reduce the heat and simmer for about 15 minutes, or until the potatoes are tender.
5. **Make it Creamy:**
    - Stir in the heavy cream and milk. If you prefer a thicker chowder, you can mix the flour with a bit of milk to make a slurry and add it to the pot at this stage. Cook for another 5 minutes, stirring occasionally, until the chowder is heated through and slightly thickened.
6. **Add Crab Meat:**

- Gently fold in the crab meat and cook for an additional 2-3 minutes, just until the crab is heated through. Be careful not to over-stir or break up the crab meat too much.
7. **Season and Finish:**
    - Stir in the lemon juice and season with salt and black pepper to taste.
    - Remove the bay leaf.
8. **Serve:**
    - Ladle the chowder into bowls.
    - Garnish with the reserved crispy bacon and chopped fresh parsley.

Enjoy your creamy and flavorful Corn and Crab Chowder!

Bahamian Conch Salad

Ingredients:

- 1 pound conch meat (fresh or frozen, cleaned and diced)
- 1 cup diced red bell pepper
- 1 cup diced green bell pepper
- 1 cup diced cucumber
- 1 cup diced tomatoes
- ½ cup finely chopped red onion
- ¼ cup chopped fresh cilantro or parsley
- 1-2 Scotch bonnet peppers, seeded and finely chopped (adjust to taste for heat)
- Juice of 2-3 limes (about ¼ cup)
- Juice of 1 lemon (about 2 tablespoons)
- 2 tablespoons olive oil
- 1 teaspoon sugar (optional, to balance acidity)
- Salt and black pepper to taste

Instructions:

1. **Prepare the Conch Meat:**
   - If using frozen conch, thaw it completely and rinse well.
   - For fresh conch, clean and dice it into small, bite-sized pieces.
   - Blanch the conch if necessary: Bring a pot of water to a boil, add the conch, and cook for about 2-3 minutes. Drain and rinse under cold water. This step helps to tenderize the conch.
2. **Combine the Vegetables:**
   - In a large mixing bowl, combine the diced red bell pepper, green bell pepper, cucumber, tomatoes, red onion, and Scotch bonnet peppers.
3. **Mix the Salad:**
   - Add the diced conch meat to the bowl with the vegetables.
   - Stir in the chopped cilantro or parsley.
4. **Add the Dressing:**
   - In a small bowl, whisk together the lime juice, lemon juice, olive oil, and sugar (if using).
   - Pour the dressing over the conch and vegetable mixture.
   - Toss everything together to coat evenly.
5. **Season and Serve:**
   - Season the salad with salt and black pepper to taste.
   - Let the salad sit for about 15-20 minutes before serving to allow the flavors to meld.

Enjoy your refreshing Bahamian Conch Salad, a perfect blend of tangy, spicy, and fresh flavors!

Plantain Chips

Ingredients:

- 2-3 ripe or green plantains (unripe plantains are used for a more starchy, less sweet chip)
- Vegetable oil (for frying)
- Salt (to taste)
- Optional: other seasonings like paprika, garlic powder, or cayenne pepper

Instructions:

1. **Prepare the Plantains:**
    - Peel the plantains. To do this, cut off the ends and make a slit along the length of the plantain. Use your fingers or a knife to remove the skin.
    - Slice the plantains into thin rounds (about 1/8-inch thick) or use a mandoline slicer for uniform slices.
2. **Heat the Oil:**
    - In a large, heavy-bottomed pan or deep fryer, heat about 2 inches of vegetable oil to 350°F (175°C). You can test the oil temperature by dropping a small slice of plantain into the oil; it should sizzle and rise to the surface.
3. **Fry the Plantains:**
    - Fry the plantain slices in batches, being careful not to overcrowd the pan. Fry until they are golden brown and crispy, about 2-3 minutes per batch.
    - Use a slotted spoon to transfer the fried plantains to a paper towel-lined plate to drain excess oil.
4. **Season the Chips:**
    - While the chips are still warm, sprinkle them with salt and any other desired seasonings. Toss gently to coat.
5. **Cool and Serve:**
    - Allow the plantain chips to cool completely. They will become even crispier as they cool.

Enjoy your homemade Plantain Chips as a tasty snack or appetizer!

Citrus-Marinated Grilled Fish

Ingredients:

For the Marinade:

- ½ cup fresh orange juice
- ¼ cup fresh lemon juice
- 2 tablespoons fresh lime juice
- ¼ cup olive oil
- 3 cloves garlic, minced
- 1 tablespoon honey or agave syrup
- 1 teaspoon ground cumin
- 1 teaspoon dried oregano
- 1 teaspoon smoked paprika
- ½ teaspoon salt
- ½ teaspoon black pepper
- ¼ teaspoon crushed red pepper flakes (optional, for heat)

For the Fish:

- 4 fish fillets (such as mahi-mahi, snapper, or tilapia), about 6 ounces each
- Fresh cilantro or parsley, chopped (for garnish)

Instructions:

1. **Prepare the Marinade:**
   - In a medium bowl, whisk together the orange juice, lemon juice, lime juice, olive oil, minced garlic, honey, ground cumin, dried oregano, smoked paprika, salt, black pepper, and crushed red pepper flakes (if using).
2. **Marinate the Fish:**
   - Place the fish fillets in a large resealable plastic bag or a shallow dish.
   - Pour the marinade over the fish, ensuring all fillets are well-coated.
   - Seal the bag or cover the dish and refrigerate for 30 minutes to 1 hour. Do not marinate for too long, as the citrus can start to "cook" the fish.
3. **Preheat the Grill:**
   - Preheat your grill to medium-high heat.
4. **Grill the Fish:**
   - Remove the fish from the marinade and discard the marinade.
   - Lightly oil the grill grates or brush the fish with a bit of oil to prevent sticking.
   - Place the fish fillets on the grill and cook for about 3-5 minutes per side, or until the fish is opaque and flakes easily with a fork. Cooking time will vary depending on the thickness of the fillets.
5. **Serve:**
   - Transfer the grilled fish to a serving platter.

- Garnish with chopped fresh cilantro or parsley.

Enjoy your Citrus-Marinated Grilled Fish with your favorite sides such as a fresh salad, rice, or grilled vegetables!

Cuban Arroz con Pollo

Ingredients:

- 1 whole chicken (about 3-4 pounds), cut into pieces (or 4-6 bone-in, skinless chicken thighs/drumsticks)
- 2 tablespoons olive oil
- 1 large onion, chopped
- 1 bell pepper (red or green), chopped
- 4 cloves garlic, minced
- 1 cup long-grain rice (such as jasmine or basmati)
- 1 cup frozen peas (or fresh peas if available)
- 1 cup tomato sauce
- 2 cups chicken broth
- 1 cup dry white wine (optional; can substitute with additional chicken broth)
- 1 teaspoon ground cumin
- 1 teaspoon paprika
- 1 teaspoon dried oregano
- ½ teaspoon saffron threads (optional, for color and flavor)
- 1 bay leaf
- 1 cup pimento-stuffed olives, sliced
- 1 cup chopped fresh cilantro (for garnish)
- 1 lemon, cut into wedges (for serving)

Instructions:

1. **Prepare the Chicken:**
   - Season the chicken pieces with salt and black pepper.
2. **Brown the Chicken:**
   - In a large pot or Dutch oven, heat the olive oil over medium-high heat.
   - Add the chicken pieces and cook until browned on all sides, about 5-7 minutes. Remove the chicken and set aside.
3. **Sauté the Aromatics:**
   - In the same pot, add the chopped onion and bell pepper. Cook until softened, about 5 minutes.
   - Add the minced garlic and cook for an additional 1-2 minutes until fragrant.
4. **Add Rice and Spices:**
   - Stir in the rice, ground cumin, paprika, dried oregano, and saffron threads (if using). Cook for 2 minutes, allowing the rice to toast slightly and absorb the spices.
5. **Add Liquids and Chicken:**
   - Stir in the tomato sauce, chicken broth, and white wine (if using).
   - Add the bay leaf and olives.
   - Return the browned chicken to the pot, placing it on top of the rice mixture.

6. **Cook the Dish:**
    - Bring the mixture to a boil, then reduce the heat to low.
    - Cover and simmer for 30-40 minutes, or until the rice is cooked and the chicken is tender. Stir occasionally and check the liquid level; add a bit more broth if needed.
7. **Add Peas:**
    - About 10 minutes before the cooking time is up, stir in the frozen peas.
    - Continue cooking until the peas are heated through and the rice is tender.
8. **Finish and Serve:**
    - Remove the bay leaf and discard.
    - Garnish with chopped fresh cilantro.
    - Serve with lemon wedges on the side.

Enjoy your Cuban Arroz con Pollo, a comforting and hearty meal with vibrant flavors!

Florida Key Lime Cheesecake

Ingredients:

For the Crust:

- 1 ½ cups graham cracker crumbs (about 10-12 graham crackers)
- ¼ cup granulated sugar
- 6 tablespoons unsalted butter, melted

For the Filling:

- 4 (8-ounce) packages cream cheese, softened
- 1 cup granulated sugar
- 1 cup sour cream
- 4 large eggs
- 1 cup key lime juice (freshly squeezed or bottled, but make sure it's key lime juice)
- 1 tablespoon key lime zest (from about 2-3 key limes)
- 1 teaspoon vanilla extract

For the Topping (Optional):

- 1 cup heavy cream
- 2 tablespoons powdered sugar
- Key lime zest or fresh key lime slices for garnish

Instructions:

1. **Preheat the Oven:**
   - Preheat your oven to 325°F (163°C).
2. **Prepare the Crust:**
   - In a medium bowl, combine the graham cracker crumbs, granulated sugar, and melted butter. Mix until the crumbs are evenly coated and resemble wet sand.
   - Press the mixture into the bottom of a 9-inch springform pan to form an even layer. Use the back of a spoon or the bottom of a glass to press it down firmly.
   - Bake the crust in the preheated oven for about 10 minutes. Remove and let it cool while you prepare the filling.
3. **Prepare the Filling:**
   - In a large bowl, beat the softened cream cheese with an electric mixer until smooth and creamy.
   - Gradually add the granulated sugar and beat until well combined.
   - Add the sour cream and beat until incorporated.
   - Add the eggs one at a time, beating well after each addition.
   - Mix in the key lime juice, key lime zest, and vanilla extract until the mixture is smooth and well combined.

4. **Bake the Cheesecake:**
    - Pour the filling over the pre-baked graham cracker crust in the springform pan.
    - Smooth the top with a spatula.
    - Bake in the preheated oven for 55-65 minutes, or until the center is set and the edges are lightly browned. The center should still have a slight jiggle when you gently shake the pan.
    - Turn off the oven and crack the oven door slightly. Let the cheesecake cool in the oven for 1 hour.
5. **Chill the Cheesecake:**
    - After cooling, remove the cheesecake from the oven and refrigerate for at least 4 hours, preferably overnight, to fully set and chill.
6. **Prepare the Topping (Optional):**
    - In a medium bowl, beat the heavy cream with powdered sugar until stiff peaks form.
    - Spread or pipe the whipped cream over the chilled cheesecake.
7. **Garnish and Serve:**
    - Garnish with additional key lime zest or fresh key lime slices if desired.
    - Release the cheesecake from the springform pan and transfer it to a serving platter.

Enjoy your creamy and tangy Florida Key Lime Cheesecake!

Spicy Florida Prawns

Ingredients:

- 1 pound large Florida prawns, peeled and deveined (tails on or off, as preferred)
- 2 tablespoons olive oil
- 4 cloves garlic, minced
- 1 teaspoon smoked paprika
- 1 teaspoon cayenne pepper (adjust to taste for heat)
- 1 teaspoon ground cumin
- 1 teaspoon chili powder
- ½ teaspoon onion powder
- ½ teaspoon dried oregano
- ½ teaspoon salt
- ¼ teaspoon black pepper
- Juice of 1 lime
- 2 tablespoons chopped fresh parsley or cilantro (for garnish)
- Lemon or lime wedges (for serving)

Instructions:

1. **Prepare the Prawns:**
   - Rinse the prawns and pat them dry with paper towels.
   - In a large bowl, toss the prawns with the olive oil, making sure they are evenly coated.
2. **Season the Prawns:**
   - In a small bowl, mix together the minced garlic, smoked paprika, cayenne pepper, ground cumin, chili powder, onion powder, dried oregano, salt, and black pepper.
   - Sprinkle the spice mixture over the prawns and toss to coat evenly.
3. **Cook the Prawns:**
   - **Grilling:**
     - Preheat your grill to medium-high heat.
     - Thread the prawns onto skewers if desired for easier handling.
     - Grill the prawns for 2-3 minutes per side, or until they turn pink and opaque, and have nice grill marks.
   - **Sautéing:**
     - Heat a large skillet over medium-high heat.
     - Add the seasoned prawns to the hot skillet.
     - Sauté for about 2-3 minutes per side, or until the prawns are pink and opaque, and the spices are fragrant.
4. **Finish the Dish:**
   - Remove the prawns from the heat and squeeze lime juice over them.
   - Garnish with chopped fresh parsley or cilantro.

5. **Serve:**
    - Serve the spicy Florida prawns hot with lemon or lime wedges on the side.

Enjoy your flavorful and spicy Florida Prawns as a delicious appetizer or part of a main meal!

Key West Lime Marinade

Ingredients:

- ½ cup fresh Key lime juice (or regular lime juice if Key limes are not available)
- ¼ cup olive oil
- 3 cloves garlic, minced
- 1 tablespoon honey or agave syrup
- 1 tablespoon soy sauce
- 1 teaspoon ground cumin
- 1 teaspoon dried oregano
- 1 teaspoon paprika
- ½ teaspoon crushed red pepper flakes (optional, for heat)
- Salt and black pepper to taste
- 2 tablespoons fresh cilantro or parsley, chopped (optional, for added flavor)

Instructions:

1. **Mix the Marinade:**
   - In a medium bowl, whisk together the fresh lime juice, olive oil, minced garlic, honey, and soy sauce.
2. **Add Spices:**
   - Stir in the ground cumin, dried oregano, paprika, and crushed red pepper flakes (if using).
   - Season with salt and black pepper to taste.
3. **Optional: Add Fresh Herbs:**
   - If using, mix in the chopped fresh cilantro or parsley for added freshness and flavor.
4. **Marinate:**
   - Place your protein (chicken, fish, etc.) or vegetables in a resealable plastic bag or shallow dish.
   - Pour the marinade over the top, ensuring everything is well-coated.
   - Seal the bag or cover the dish and refrigerate for at least 30 minutes, ideally 2-4 hours, to let the flavors infuse.
5. **Cook:**
   - Remove the protein or vegetables from the marinade and discard the marinade.
   - Grill, bake, or sauté according to your recipe.

Enjoy your Key West Lime Marinade and the bright, zesty flavor it brings to your dishes!

Cuban Ropa Vieja

Ingredients:

- **For the Beef:**
    - 2 pounds flank steak or skirt steak
    - 1 onion, quartered
    - 4 cloves garlic, peeled
    - 2 bay leaves
    - 1 teaspoon dried oregano
    - 1 teaspoon ground cumin
    - Salt and black pepper to taste
- **For the Ropa Vieja:**
    - 2 tablespoons olive oil
    - 1 large onion, thinly sliced
    - 1 bell pepper (red or green), thinly sliced
    - 4 cloves garlic, minced
    - 1 can (14.5 ounces) diced tomatoes
    - ¼ cup tomato paste
    - ½ cup dry white wine (optional; can substitute with beef broth)
    - 1 cup beef broth
    - 1 teaspoon ground cumin
    - 1 teaspoon dried oregano
    - 1 teaspoon smoked paprika
    - ½ teaspoon ground black pepper
    - 1 bay leaf
    - ¼ cup pimento-stuffed olives, sliced
    - 2 tablespoons capers, rinsed and drained
    - 2 tablespoons fresh cilantro or parsley, chopped (for garnish)

Instructions:

1. **Cook the Beef:**
    - In a large pot or Dutch oven, place the flank steak, onion, garlic, bay leaves, dried oregano, ground cumin, salt, and black pepper.
    - Cover with water and bring to a boil.
    - Reduce heat and simmer for 2-3 hours, or until the beef is tender and easily shreds. Alternatively, you can use a slow cooker on low for 6-8 hours.
    - Remove the beef from the pot and let it cool slightly. Discard the bay leaves, onion, and garlic.
    - Shred the beef into thin strips using two forks.
2. **Prepare the Ropa Vieja Sauce:**
    - In the same pot or a large skillet, heat the olive oil over medium heat.
    - Add the sliced onion and bell pepper. Cook until softened, about 5-7 minutes.

- Add the minced garlic and cook for an additional 1-2 minutes until fragrant.
- Stir in the diced tomatoes, tomato paste, and white wine (if using). Cook for 2-3 minutes to combine.
- Add the beef broth, ground cumin, dried oregano, smoked paprika, ground black pepper, and bay leaf. Stir to combine.
- Return the shredded beef to the pot. Stir to coat the beef with the sauce.
- Reduce heat to low and simmer for 30-45 minutes, allowing the flavors to meld and the sauce to thicken. Stir occasionally.

3. **Finish and Serve:**
    - Stir in the sliced olives and capers.
    - Adjust seasoning with salt and pepper if needed.
    - Garnish with chopped fresh cilantro or parsley.

4. **Serving Suggestions:**
    - Serve Ropa Vieja over rice with black beans, fried plantains, or a side of Cuban bread.

Enjoy this savory and satisfying Cuban classic!

Grilled Shrimp Skewers

Ingredients:

- **For the Marinade:**
    - ¼ cup olive oil
    - 3 tablespoons fresh lemon juice
    - 3 cloves garlic, minced
    - 1 tablespoon fresh parsley or cilantro, chopped (optional)
    - 1 teaspoon dried oregano
    - 1 teaspoon smoked paprika
    - ½ teaspoon ground cumin
    - ½ teaspoon red pepper flakes (adjust to taste for heat)
    - Salt and black pepper to taste
- **For the Shrimp:**
    - 1 pound large shrimp (16-20 count), peeled and deveined (tails on or off, as preferred)
    - Lemon wedges (for serving)
    - Fresh parsley or cilantro (for garnish)

Instructions:

1. **Prepare the Marinade:**
    - In a medium bowl, whisk together the olive oil, lemon juice, minced garlic, parsley or cilantro (if using), dried oregano, smoked paprika, ground cumin, red pepper flakes, salt, and black pepper.
2. **Marinate the Shrimp:**
    - Place the shrimp in a large resealable plastic bag or shallow dish.
    - Pour the marinade over the shrimp and toss to coat evenly.
    - Seal the bag or cover the dish and refrigerate for 30 minutes to 1 hour. Do not marinate for too long as the acidity can begin to "cook" the shrimp.
3. **Preheat the Grill:**
    - Preheat your grill to medium-high heat (about 375°F to 400°F or 190°C to 200°C).
4. **Prepare the Skewers:**
    - If using wooden skewers, soak them in water for at least 30 minutes to prevent burning.
    - Thread the marinated shrimp onto the skewers, leaving a bit of space between each shrimp for even cooking.
5. **Grill the Shrimp:**
    - Place the skewers on the grill and cook for 2-3 minutes per side, or until the shrimp are pink and opaque. Be careful not to overcook them as shrimp can become tough if cooked too long.
6. **Serve:**

- Remove the shrimp from the grill and transfer them to a serving platter.
- Garnish with additional chopped fresh parsley or cilantro and serve with lemon wedges.

Serving Suggestions:

- Serve the grilled shrimp skewers over a bed of rice, alongside a fresh salad, or with grilled vegetables.

Enjoy your flavorful and perfectly grilled shrimp skewers!

Florida Mango Salsa

Ingredients:

- 2 ripe Florida mangos, peeled, pitted, and diced
- 1 small red bell pepper, diced
- 1 small red onion, finely diced
- 1 jalapeño pepper, seeded and finely chopped (adjust to taste for heat)
- ¼ cup fresh cilantro, chopped
- Juice of 1 lime
- 1 tablespoon honey or agave syrup (optional, for extra sweetness)
- Salt and black pepper to taste

Instructions:

1. **Prepare the Ingredients:**
    - Dice the mangos, red bell pepper, and red onion into small, uniform pieces.
    - Seed and finely chop the jalapeño pepper.
    - Chop the fresh cilantro.
2. **Combine the Ingredients:**
    - In a large bowl, gently combine the diced mangos, red bell pepper, red onion, jalapeño pepper, and cilantro.
3. **Add the Dressing:**
    - Squeeze the lime juice over the salsa mixture.
    - If using, drizzle in the honey or agave syrup for a touch of extra sweetness.
    - Season with salt and black pepper to taste.
4. **Mix and Chill:**
    - Gently toss everything together to combine.
    - Let the salsa sit for at least 15-30 minutes to allow the flavors to meld.
5. **Serve:**
    - Serve the mango salsa as a topping for grilled fish, chicken, or tacos, or with tortilla chips as a dip.

Enjoy your vibrant and tangy Florida Mango Salsa!

Southern Fried Catfish

Ingredients:

- **For the Catfish:**
    - 4 catfish fillets (about 6 ounces each), skinless and boneless
    - 1 cup buttermilk
    - 1 cup all-purpose flour
    - ½ cup cornmeal
    - 1 teaspoon paprika
    - 1 teaspoon garlic powder
    - 1 teaspoon onion powder
    - ½ teaspoon cayenne pepper (adjust to taste for heat)
    - ½ teaspoon dried thyme
    - ½ teaspoon dried oregano
    - 1 teaspoon salt
    - ½ teaspoon black pepper
- **For Frying:**
    - Vegetable oil (such as canola or peanut oil), for frying

Instructions:

1. **Prepare the Catfish:**
    - Rinse the catfish fillets under cold water and pat them dry with paper towels.
    - Place the fillets in a shallow dish and pour the buttermilk over them. Let them soak in the buttermilk for at least 30 minutes. This helps to tenderize the fish and gives the coating something to adhere to.
2. **Prepare the Coating:**
    - In a large bowl, combine the flour, cornmeal, paprika, garlic powder, onion powder, cayenne pepper, dried thyme, dried oregano, salt, and black pepper. Mix well.
3. **Dredge the Fillets:**
    - Remove the catfish fillets from the buttermilk, allowing any excess to drip off.
    - Dredge each fillet in the flour and cornmeal mixture, coating both sides evenly. Press down lightly to ensure the coating sticks.
4. **Heat the Oil:**
    - In a large skillet or deep fryer, heat about 1-2 inches of vegetable oil to 350°F (175°C). You can test the oil temperature by dropping a small piece of bread into the oil; it should sizzle and turn golden brown.
5. **Fry the Catfish:**
    - Carefully place the coated catfish fillets in the hot oil. Fry in batches, if necessary, to avoid overcrowding the pan.

- Cook the fillets for about 3-4 minutes per side, or until they are golden brown and crispy. The internal temperature of the fish should reach 145°F (63°C), and the fish should flake easily with a fork.
6. **Drain and Serve:**
    - Remove the fried catfish from the oil and place them on a plate lined with paper towels to drain any excess oil.
    - Serve hot with your favorite sides, such as coleslaw, cornbread, or fries.

Tips:

- **For Extra Crispy Coating:** Let the coated fish rest for about 10-15 minutes before frying. This helps the coating adhere better.
- **For a Spicier Kick:** Adjust the amount of cayenne pepper or add hot sauce to the buttermilk for an extra layer of heat.

Enjoy your Southern Fried Catfish with classic sides for a hearty, delicious meal!

Florida Citrus Salad

Ingredients:

- **For the Salad:**
    - 1 large grapefruit, peeled and segmented
    - 2 large oranges, peeled and segmented (use navel or blood oranges for best flavor)
    - 1 large avocado, peeled, pitted, and sliced
    - 1 cup baby spinach or mixed greens
    - ¼ cup red onion, thinly sliced
    - ¼ cup crumbled feta cheese or goat cheese (optional)
    - ¼ cup toasted almonds or pecans (optional)
    - Fresh mint or basil leaves for garnish (optional)
- **For the Citrus Vinaigrette:**
    - ¼ cup fresh orange juice
    - 2 tablespoons fresh lemon juice
    - 1 tablespoon fresh lime juice
    - ¼ cup extra-virgin olive oil
    - 1 tablespoon honey or agave syrup
    - 1 teaspoon Dijon mustard
    - Salt and black pepper to taste

Instructions:

1. **Prepare the Citrus:**
    - Peel and segment the grapefruit and oranges, removing any seeds and membrane.
    - To segment, use a sharp knife to cut between the membranes of the citrus fruit to release the individual segments.
2. **Assemble the Salad:**
    - In a large salad bowl or platter, arrange the baby spinach or mixed greens as the base.
    - Scatter the citrus segments, avocado slices, and red onion over the greens.
    - Sprinkle with crumbled feta cheese or goat cheese and toasted almonds or pecans if using.
3. **Prepare the Citrus Vinaigrette:**
    - In a small bowl or jar, whisk together the orange juice, lemon juice, lime juice, olive oil, honey or agave syrup, and Dijon mustard until well combined.
    - Season with salt and black pepper to taste.
4. **Dress the Salad:**
    - Drizzle the citrus vinaigrette over the salad just before serving.
    - Toss gently to combine, or leave the vinaigrette on the side for guests to add as they prefer.

5. **Garnish and Serve:**
    - Garnish with fresh mint or basil leaves if desired.
    - Serve immediately for the freshest flavor and best texture.

Tips:

- **For Added Flavor:** You can add thinly sliced radishes or cucumber for extra crunch.
- **For a Protein Boost:** Top with grilled chicken or shrimp for a more substantial meal.

Enjoy your Florida Citrus Salad as a refreshing and zesty addition to any meal!

Mojo Chicken Wings

Ingredients:

- **For the Mojo Marinade:**
    - ½ cup fresh orange juice
    - ¼ cup fresh lime juice
    - ¼ cup olive oil
    - 6 cloves garlic, minced
    - 1 tablespoon fresh oregano (or 1 teaspoon dried oregano)
    - 1 teaspoon ground cumin
    - 1 teaspoon smoked paprika
    - 1 teaspoon dried thyme
    - ½ teaspoon crushed red pepper flakes (adjust to taste for heat)
    - 1 teaspoon salt
    - ½ teaspoon black pepper
- **For the Chicken Wings:**
    - 2 pounds chicken wings, separated into flats and drumettes
    - Fresh cilantro or parsley, chopped (for garnish)
    - Lime wedges (for serving)

Instructions:

1. **Prepare the Mojo Marinade:**
    - In a medium bowl, whisk together the orange juice, lime juice, olive oil, minced garlic, oregano, ground cumin, smoked paprika, dried thyme, crushed red pepper flakes, salt, and black pepper.
2. **Marinate the Chicken Wings:**
    - Place the chicken wings in a large resealable plastic bag or shallow dish.
    - Pour the mojo marinade over the wings and toss to coat evenly.
    - Seal the bag or cover the dish and refrigerate for at least 2 hours, preferably overnight, to allow the flavors to infuse.
3. **Preheat the Oven or Grill:**
    - **Oven Method:** Preheat your oven to 400°F (200°C). Line a baking sheet with parchment paper or aluminum foil and place a wire rack on top of the sheet.
    - **Grill Method:** Preheat your grill to medium-high heat.
4. **Cook the Chicken Wings:**
    - **Oven Method:**
        - Remove the wings from the marinade and arrange them in a single layer on the wire rack.
        - Bake for 35-45 minutes, or until the wings are golden brown and crispy, flipping them halfway through the cooking time.
    - **Grill Method:**
        - Remove the wings from the marinade and place them on the grill.

- Grill for about 20-25 minutes, turning occasionally, until the wings are cooked through and have a nice char.

5. **Serve:**
    - Transfer the cooked wings to a serving platter.
    - Garnish with chopped fresh cilantro or parsley.
    - Serve with lime wedges on the side for an extra burst of citrus.

Tips:

- **For Extra Crispiness:** Pat the wings dry with paper towels before marinating and avoid overcrowding them on the baking sheet or grill.
- **For a Spicier Kick:** Add more crushed red pepper flakes or a dash of hot sauce to the marinade.

Enjoy your Mojo Chicken Wings with their bright and tangy flavors that are sure to be a hit!

Gator Gumbo

Ingredients:

- **For the Gumbo:**
    - 1 pound alligator meat, cut into bite-sized pieces (or substitute with chicken or sausage)
    - ¼ cup vegetable oil
    - ¼ cup all-purpose flour
    - 1 large onion, chopped
    - 1 bell pepper (red or green), chopped
    - 3 cloves garlic, minced
    - 3 celery stalks, chopped
    - 1 can (14.5 ounces) diced tomatoes
    - 4 cups chicken broth
    - 2 cups water
    - 2 bay leaves
    - 1 teaspoon dried thyme
    - 1 teaspoon paprika
    - 1 teaspoon ground cumin
    - 1 teaspoon dried oregano
    - ½ teaspoon cayenne pepper (adjust to taste for heat)
    - Salt and black pepper to taste
    - 1 cup sliced andouille sausage (optional)
    - 1 cup okra, sliced (fresh or frozen)
    - 1 tablespoon Worcestershire sauce
    - 2 tablespoons fresh parsley, chopped (for garnish)
    - Cooked white rice (for serving)

Instructions:

1. **Prepare the Roux:**
    - In a large pot or Dutch oven, heat the vegetable oil over medium heat.
    - Gradually whisk in the flour, creating a roux. Cook, stirring constantly, for about 10-15 minutes, or until the roux is a deep brown color. Be careful not to burn it.
2. **Cook the Vegetables:**
    - Add the chopped onion, bell pepper, garlic, and celery to the roux. Cook for about 5-7 minutes, or until the vegetables are softened.
3. **Add the Liquids and Seasonings:**
    - Stir in the diced tomatoes, chicken broth, and water.
    - Add the bay leaves, dried thyme, paprika, ground cumin, dried oregano, cayenne pepper, salt, and black pepper.
    - Bring the mixture to a boil, then reduce the heat to low.
4. **Simmer the Gumbo:**

- Add the alligator meat (or chicken) and sausage (if using) to the pot.
- Cover and simmer for about 45 minutes to 1 hour, or until the meat is tender and the flavors are well combined.

5. **Add Okra and Worcestershire Sauce:**
    - Stir in the okra and Worcestershire sauce.
    - Continue to simmer for an additional 10-15 minutes, or until the okra is tender and the gumbo has thickened.
6. **Finish and Serve:**
    - Remove the bay leaves.
    - Adjust seasoning with additional salt and pepper if needed.
    - Serve the gumbo over cooked white rice.
    - Garnish with chopped fresh parsley.

Tips:

- **For a Thicker Gumbo:** If you prefer a thicker gumbo, you can add more okra or simmer the gumbo uncovered for a longer period.
- **For Extra Flavor:** Try adding a splash of hot sauce or additional spices to suit your taste.

Enjoy your flavorful and comforting Gator Gumbo!

Blackened Red Snapper

Ingredients:

- **For the Blackened Seasoning:**
    - 1 tablespoon paprika
    - 1 teaspoon dried oregano
    - 1 teaspoon dried thyme
    - 1 teaspoon garlic powder
    - 1 teaspoon onion powder
    - ½ teaspoon cayenne pepper (adjust to taste for heat)
    - ½ teaspoon ground cumin
    - ½ teaspoon smoked paprika (for extra smoky flavor)
    - ½ teaspoon salt
    - ½ teaspoon black pepper
- **For the Red Snapper:**
    - 4 red snapper fillets (about 6 ounces each)
    - 2 tablespoons melted butter or olive oil (for brushing)
    - Lemon wedges (for serving)
    - Fresh parsley or cilantro, chopped (for garnish)

Instructions:

1. **Prepare the Blackened Seasoning:**
    - In a small bowl, combine the paprika, dried oregano, dried thyme, garlic powder, onion powder, cayenne pepper, ground cumin, smoked paprika, salt, and black pepper.
    - Mix well to combine.
2. **Season the Fish:**
    - Pat the red snapper fillets dry with paper towels.
    - Brush each fillet lightly with melted butter or olive oil.
    - Generously coat both sides of each fillet with the blackened seasoning, pressing gently to ensure it sticks.
3. **Preheat the Pan:**
    - Heat a large cast-iron skillet or heavy-bottomed skillet over high heat until it is very hot and smoking slightly. You can also use a grill pan if preferred.
4. **Cook the Red Snapper:**
    - Place the seasoned fillets in the hot skillet. Cook for about 2-3 minutes per side, or until the fish is blackened and crispy on the outside and flakes easily with a fork. Be careful not to overcrowd the pan; cook in batches if necessary.
5. **Serve:**
    - Transfer the blackened red snapper fillets to a serving platter.
    - Garnish with fresh parsley or cilantro.
    - Serve with lemon wedges on the side for squeezing over the fish.

Tips:

- **For a More Intense Flavor:** You can marinate the fish in a bit of lemon juice and a portion of the blackened seasoning for 30 minutes before cooking.
- **Adjust the Spice Level:** Feel free to adjust the amount of cayenne pepper and black pepper to suit your taste.

Enjoy your Blackened Red Snapper with your favorite sides for a flavorful and satisfying meal!

Florida Style Fried Chicken

Ingredients:

- **For the Chicken:**
    - 3 pounds chicken pieces (legs, thighs, breasts, or a mix), bone-in and skin-on
    - 1 cup buttermilk
    - 1 tablespoon hot sauce (optional, for extra flavor)
- **For the Flour Coating:**
    - 1 cup all-purpose flour
    - 1 cup cornmeal
    - 1 tablespoon paprika
    - 1 teaspoon garlic powder
    - 1 teaspoon onion powder
    - 1 teaspoon dried thyme
    - 1 teaspoon dried oregano
    - 1 teaspoon salt
    - ½ teaspoon black pepper
    - ½ teaspoon cayenne pepper (adjust to taste for heat)
- **For Frying:**
    - Vegetable oil (such as canola or peanut oil), for frying
- **For Citrus Brine (optional but recommended):**
    - 1 cup orange juice
    - ¼ cup lemon juice
    - 2 tablespoons salt
    - 2 tablespoons sugar
    - 1 teaspoon dried thyme
    - 1 teaspoon dried oregano

Instructions:

1. **Prepare the Citrus Brine (Optional):**
    - In a large bowl, mix together the orange juice, lemon juice, salt, sugar, dried thyme, and dried oregano until the salt and sugar are dissolved.
    - Add the chicken pieces to the brine and refrigerate for 1-2 hours. This step adds a touch of Florida's citrus flavor and helps tenderize the chicken.
2. **Prepare the Chicken:**
    - If you did not use the citrus brine, skip to the marination step.
    - After brining, remove the chicken from the brine and pat it dry with paper towels.
3. **Marinate the Chicken:**
    - Place the chicken pieces in a large bowl or resealable plastic bag.
    - Pour the buttermilk and hot sauce (if using) over the chicken. Toss to coat.
    - Cover and refrigerate for at least 1 hour, or overnight for best results.
4. **Prepare the Flour Coating:**

- In a large bowl, combine the flour, cornmeal, paprika, garlic powder, onion powder, dried thyme, dried oregano, salt, black pepper, and cayenne pepper. Mix well.

5. **Coat the Chicken:**
   - Remove each piece of chicken from the buttermilk and let any excess drip off.
   - Dredge the chicken pieces in the flour mixture, pressing down to ensure an even coating. Shake off any excess flour.

6. **Heat the Oil:**
   - In a large skillet or deep fryer, heat about 2 inches of vegetable oil to 350°F (175°C). You can test the oil temperature by dropping in a small piece of bread; it should sizzle and turn golden brown.

7. **Fry the Chicken:**
   - Carefully add the coated chicken pieces to the hot oil, working in batches if necessary to avoid overcrowding the pan.
   - Fry the chicken for 10-15 minutes per side, or until the coating is golden brown and crispy, and the internal temperature reaches 165°F (74°C).

8. **Drain and Serve:**
   - Remove the chicken from the oil and place it on a plate lined with paper towels to drain any excess oil.
   - Serve hot with your favorite sides such as coleslaw, cornbread, or fried green tomatoes.

Tips:

- **For Extra Crispy Chicken:** Let the coated chicken rest for about 15 minutes before frying. This helps the coating adhere better and become crispier.
- **For Spicy Variation:** Increase the amount of cayenne pepper or add a pinch of hot sauce to the flour mixture.

Enjoy your flavorful and crispy Florida Style Fried Chicken!

Pineapple Coconut Cake

Ingredients:

- **For the Cake:**
    - 1 ¾ cups all-purpose flour
    - 1 cup granulated sugar
    - ½ cup unsweetened shredded coconut
    - ½ cup crushed pineapple, drained
    - ½ cup unsalted butter, softened
    - 2 large eggs
    - 1 cup buttermilk
    - 1 teaspoon baking powder
    - ½ teaspoon baking soda
    - ½ teaspoon salt
    - 1 teaspoon vanilla extract
- **For the Pineapple Coconut Glaze:**
    - 1 cup powdered sugar
    - 2 tablespoons unsalted butter, melted
    - 2 tablespoons pineapple juice
    - 2 tablespoons sweetened shredded coconut
- **For Garnish (optional):**
    - Additional shredded coconut
    - Pineapple slices or maraschino cherries

Instructions:

1. **Preheat the Oven:**
    - Preheat your oven to 350°F (175°C).
    - Grease and flour a 9-inch round cake pan or line it with parchment paper.
2. **Prepare the Cake Batter:**
    - In a medium bowl, whisk together the flour, baking powder, baking soda, and salt. Set aside.
    - In a large mixing bowl, cream together the softened butter and granulated sugar until light and fluffy.
    - Beat in the eggs one at a time, mixing well after each addition.
    - Add the vanilla extract and mix until combined.
    - Gradually add the flour mixture to the butter mixture, alternating with the buttermilk, beginning and ending with the flour mixture. Mix until just combined.
    - Fold in the shredded coconut and crushed pineapple until evenly distributed.
3. **Bake the Cake:**
    - Pour the batter into the prepared cake pan and smooth the top.
    - Bake for 30-35 minutes, or until a toothpick inserted into the center of the cake comes out clean.

- Let the cake cool in the pan for 10 minutes, then transfer it to a wire rack to cool completely.
4. **Prepare the Pineapple Coconut Glaze:**
    - In a small bowl, whisk together the powdered sugar, melted butter, and pineapple juice until smooth.
    - Stir in the shredded coconut.
5. **Glaze the Cake:**
    - Once the cake is completely cooled, drizzle the pineapple coconut glaze evenly over the top of the cake.
6. **Garnish and Serve:**
    - If desired, garnish with additional shredded coconut and pineapple slices or maraschino cherries.
    - Slice and serve.

Tips:

- **For Extra Moistness:** You can add a bit of the drained pineapple juice to the batter.
- **For a Coconutty Touch:** Toast the shredded coconut before using it in the glaze for added flavor and texture.

Enjoy your Pineapple Coconut Cake, a sweet and tropical treat that's perfect for any occasion!

Bahamian Johnny Cake

Ingredients:

- 2 cups all-purpose flour
- ¼ cup granulated sugar
- 2 teaspoons baking powder
- ½ teaspoon salt
- ¼ cup cold unsalted butter, cut into small pieces
- ¾ cup milk (whole or 2%)
- 1 large egg

Instructions:

1. **Preheat the Oven:**
   - Preheat your oven to 375°F (190°C).
   - Grease a 9-inch round cake pan or an 8x8-inch square baking dish, or line it with parchment paper.
2. **Prepare the Dry Ingredients:**
   - In a large mixing bowl, whisk together the flour, sugar, baking powder, and salt.
3. **Cut in the Butter:**
   - Add the cold butter pieces to the flour mixture.
   - Using a pastry cutter or your fingers, cut the butter into the flour mixture until it resembles coarse crumbs.
4. **Mix the Wet Ingredients:**
   - In a separate bowl, whisk together the milk and egg.
5. **Combine Ingredients:**
   - Pour the milk and egg mixture into the flour mixture.
   - Stir until just combined; the batter will be thick and slightly lumpy. Do not overmix.
6. **Bake the Johnny Cake:**
   - Pour the batter into the prepared baking pan and spread it out evenly.
   - Bake for 25-30 minutes, or until the top is golden brown and a toothpick inserted into the center comes out clean.
7. **Cool and Serve:**
   - Allow the Johnny Cake to cool in the pan for a few minutes before transferring it to a wire rack to cool completely.
   - Slice into squares or wedges and serve warm.

Tips:

- **For Extra Flavor:** You can add a touch of vanilla extract or a sprinkle of cinnamon to the batter.
- **For a Richer Taste:** Substitute some of the milk with coconut milk for a hint of coconut flavor.

Enjoy your Bahamian Johnny Cake as a delicious and comforting addition to your meal!

Florida-Style BBQ Shrimp

Ingredients:

- **For the Shrimp:**
    - 1 pound large shrimp, peeled and deveined (tails on or off, as preferred)
    - 2 tablespoons olive oil
    - 2 tablespoons lemon juice
    - 1 teaspoon garlic powder
    - 1 teaspoon smoked paprika
    - 1 teaspoon dried oregano
    - ½ teaspoon salt
    - ½ teaspoon black pepper
- **For the BBQ Sauce:**
    - 1 cup ketchup
    - ¼ cup brown sugar
    - ¼ cup apple cider vinegar
    - 2 tablespoons Worcestershire sauce
    - 1 tablespoon Dijon mustard
    - 1 tablespoon hot sauce (adjust to taste)
    - 1 teaspoon smoked paprika
    - 1 teaspoon garlic powder
    - ½ teaspoon onion powder
    - ½ teaspoon ground cumin
    - Salt and black pepper to taste

Instructions:

1. **Prepare the BBQ Sauce:**
    - In a medium saucepan, combine the ketchup, brown sugar, apple cider vinegar, Worcestershire sauce, Dijon mustard, hot sauce, smoked paprika, garlic powder, onion powder, and ground cumin.
    - Bring the mixture to a simmer over medium heat, stirring occasionally.
    - Reduce the heat and let the sauce simmer for about 10 minutes, or until it has thickened slightly.
    - Season with salt and black pepper to taste. Remove from heat and set aside.
2. **Prepare the Shrimp:**
    - In a large bowl, toss the shrimp with olive oil, lemon juice, garlic powder, smoked paprika, dried oregano, salt, and black pepper until evenly coated.
3. **Grill the Shrimp:**
    - Preheat your grill to medium-high heat.
    - Thread the shrimp onto skewers (if using wooden skewers, make sure they have been soaked in water for 30 minutes to prevent burning).

- Grill the shrimp for about 2-3 minutes per side, or until they are opaque and cooked through.
4. **Glaze the Shrimp:**
    - During the last minute of grilling, brush the BBQ sauce over the shrimp, allowing it to caramelize slightly.
    - Turn the shrimp to ensure they are evenly coated and caramelized.
5. **Serve:**
    - Remove the shrimp from the grill and transfer them to a serving platter.
    - Serve with extra BBQ sauce on the side for dipping.

Tips:

- **For Extra Flavor:** Marinate the shrimp in a bit of the BBQ sauce for 30 minutes before grilling for a deeper flavor.
- **For a Smoky Touch:** Add wood chips to the grill for a smokier flavor.

Enjoy your Florida-Style BBQ Shrimp as a delicious and flavorful dish perfect for any occasion!

Sweet Plantain Casserole

Ingredients:

- **For the Casserole:**
    - 4-5 ripe plantains (yellow with black spots, or slightly overripe)
    - 2 tablespoons unsalted butter, melted
    - ¼ cup brown sugar
    - 1 teaspoon ground cinnamon
    - ½ teaspoon ground nutmeg
    - 1 cup shredded sharp cheddar cheese (or a cheese of your choice)
    - ½ cup chopped pecans or walnuts (optional)
    - ½ cup raisins or dried cranberries (optional)
    - 1 large egg
    - 1 cup milk (whole or 2%)
- **For Garnish (optional):**
    - Additional chopped nuts
    - Fresh herbs like cilantro or parsley

Instructions:

1. **Preheat the Oven:**
    - Preheat your oven to 375°F (190°C).
    - Grease a 9x13-inch baking dish or a similar-sized casserole dish.
2. **Prepare the Plantains:**
    - Peel the plantains and slice them into ¼-inch thick rounds.
    - In a large bowl, toss the plantain slices with melted butter until well coated.
3. **Mix the Sweet Ingredients:**
    - In a small bowl, mix together the brown sugar, ground cinnamon, and ground nutmeg.
    - Sprinkle the mixture over the plantain slices and toss to coat evenly.
4. **Assemble the Casserole:**
    - Arrange a layer of plantain slices in the bottom of the prepared baking dish.
    - If using, sprinkle half of the chopped nuts and raisins or dried cranberries over the plantains.
    - Add another layer of plantains and top with the remaining nuts and raisins or cranberries.
5. **Prepare the Egg Mixture:**
    - In a medium bowl, whisk together the egg and milk until well combined.
    - Pour the egg mixture evenly over the layered plantains in the baking dish.
6. **Add Cheese:**
    - Sprinkle the shredded cheese evenly over the top of the casserole.
7. **Bake the Casserole:**

- Bake for 30-35 minutes, or until the plantains are tender, the casserole is set, and the cheese is melted and bubbly.
8. **Garnish and Serve:**
    - If desired, garnish with additional chopped nuts and fresh herbs.
    - Serve warm as a side dish or a sweet treat.

Tips:

- **For Extra Creaminess:** You can add a splash of heavy cream to the egg mixture for a richer texture.
- **For a Crunchy Topping:** Mix some breadcrumbs with a bit of melted butter and sprinkle on top before baking for added crunch.

Enjoy your Sweet Plantain Casserole as a delicious and unique addition to your meal!

Caribbean Jerk Pork

Ingredients:

- **For the Jerk Marinade:**
    - 1 tablespoon allspice berries (or 1 tablespoon ground allspice if unavailable)
    - 1 teaspoon dried thyme (or 2 teaspoons fresh thyme)
    - 1 teaspoon cinnamon
    - 1 teaspoon nutmeg
    - 2-4 Scotch bonnet peppers (or habanero peppers), seeds removed (adjust to taste for heat)
    - 4 cloves garlic, minced
    - 1 medium onion, chopped
    - 1 tablespoon fresh ginger, minced
    - 1/4 cup soy sauce
    - 2 tablespoons brown sugar
    - 2 tablespoons vegetable oil
    - 2 tablespoons apple cider vinegar
    - Juice of 1 lime
    - 1 teaspoon salt
    - 1 teaspoon black pepper
    - 1 teaspoon sugar (optional, for additional sweetness)
- **For the Pork:**
    - 3 pounds pork shoulder or pork loin, trimmed and cut into large chunks or slices

Instructions:

1. **Prepare the Jerk Marinade:**
    - **If using allspice berries:** Grind the allspice berries in a spice grinder or mortar and pestle until finely ground.
    - In a blender or food processor, combine the allspice (ground or whole), dried thyme, cinnamon, nutmeg, Scotch bonnet peppers, garlic, onion, ginger, soy sauce, brown sugar, vegetable oil, apple cider vinegar, lime juice, salt, and black pepper.
    - Blend until smooth, adding a bit of water if necessary to help with blending.
2. **Marinate the Pork:**
    - Place the pork chunks or slices in a large resealable plastic bag or shallow dish.
    - Pour the jerk marinade over the pork, making sure it is well coated.
    - Seal the bag or cover the dish and refrigerate for at least 2 hours, preferably overnight, to allow the flavors to penetrate the meat.
3. **Cook the Pork:**
    - **Grilling Method:**
        - Preheat your grill to medium-high heat.
        - Remove the pork from the marinade and discard any excess marinade.

- Grill the pork for about 5-7 minutes per side, or until the internal temperature reaches 145°F (63°C) for pork loin or 190°F (88°C) for pork shoulder. The exterior should be well-charred and caramelized.
    - **Oven Method:**
        - Preheat your oven to 350°F (175°C).
        - Place the marinated pork on a roasting rack set over a baking sheet.
        - Roast for about 45-60 minutes, or until the pork is cooked through and reaches the appropriate internal temperature.
        - If desired, you can broil the pork for a few minutes at the end to achieve a charred exterior.
4. **Rest and Serve:**
    - Remove the pork from the grill or oven and let it rest for 10 minutes before slicing.
    - Slice the pork and serve with traditional sides such as rice and peas, fried plantains, or a fresh salad.

Tips:

- **Adjusting Heat:** Scotch bonnet peppers are very hot. Adjust the quantity based on your heat preference, or use milder peppers if desired.
- **For Extra Flavor:** Baste the pork with additional marinade or a mix of honey and soy sauce while grilling for added flavor and caramelization.

Enjoy your Caribbean Jerk Pork with its bold and authentic flavors!

Florida Key Lime Bars

Ingredients:

- **For the Crust:**
    - 1 ½ cups graham cracker crumbs (about 10-12 graham crackers)
    - ¼ cup granulated sugar
    - 6 tablespoons unsalted butter, melted
- **For the Key Lime Filling:**
    - 4 large egg yolks
    - 1 can (14 ounces) sweetened condensed milk
    - ½ cup freshly squeezed key lime juice (about 6-8 key limes) or regular lime juice
    - Zest of 2 key limes or regular limes
- **For the Whipped Cream Topping:**
    - 1 cup heavy cream
    - 2 tablespoons powdered sugar
    - 1 teaspoon vanilla extract

Instructions:

1. **Prepare the Crust:**
    - Preheat your oven to 350°F (175°C).
    - In a medium bowl, combine the graham cracker crumbs, granulated sugar, and melted butter. Mix until the crumbs are evenly coated and the mixture resembles wet sand.
    - Press the mixture firmly into the bottom of an 8x8-inch baking dish or a 9x9-inch dish lined with parchment paper or aluminum foil. Use the back of a spoon or a flat-bottomed glass to press it down evenly.
    - Bake the crust for 8-10 minutes, or until it is golden brown. Remove from the oven and let it cool slightly.
2. **Prepare the Key Lime Filling:**
    - In a large bowl, whisk together the egg yolks until slightly thickened.
    - Add the sweetened condensed milk and continue to whisk until well combined.
    - Stir in the key lime juice and zest, mixing until smooth.
    - Pour the filling over the pre-baked graham cracker crust and spread it evenly.
3. **Bake the Bars:**
    - Bake the bars in the preheated oven for 15-20 minutes, or until the filling is set and the edges are slightly puffed. The center should still have a slight jiggle.
    - Remove from the oven and let it cool to room temperature. Once cooled, refrigerate for at least 2 hours or until completely chilled and set.
4. **Prepare the Whipped Cream Topping:**
    - In a medium bowl, whip the heavy cream with an electric mixer on medium-high speed until soft peaks form.

- Add the powdered sugar and vanilla extract, and continue to whip until stiff peaks form.
5. **Assemble and Serve:**
    - Once the bars are fully chilled, spread or pipe the whipped cream over the top.
    - Garnish with additional lime zest or thin lime slices if desired.
    - Cut into squares and serve chilled.

Tips:

- **For Extra Tang:** You can adjust the amount of key lime juice to your taste preference.
- **For Easy Removal:** Line the baking dish with parchment paper, leaving an overhang on the sides to easily lift out the bars.

Enjoy your Florida Key Lime Bars for a delightful, tangy treat that's sure to impress!

Florida Fried Green Tomatoes

Ingredients:

- **For the Tomatoes:**
    - 4-5 green tomatoes (firm, unripe tomatoes)
    - 1 cup all-purpose flour
    - 1 cup cornmeal
    - 1 teaspoon salt
    - ½ teaspoon black pepper
    - 1 teaspoon paprika
    - 1 teaspoon garlic powder
    - ½ teaspoon onion powder
    - 2 large eggs
    - 1 cup buttermilk (or regular milk with a tablespoon of lemon juice added)
    - Vegetable oil (such as canola or peanut oil) for frying

Instructions:

1. **Prepare the Tomatoes:**
    - Wash and slice the green tomatoes into ¼-inch thick rounds.
    - Arrange the tomato slices on a paper towel and lightly sprinkle with salt. Let them sit for about 10 minutes to draw out excess moisture. Pat them dry with paper towels.
2. **Prepare the Breading Stations:**
    - In a shallow dish, combine the flour, cornmeal, salt, black pepper, paprika, garlic powder, and onion powder. Mix well.
    - In another shallow dish, whisk together the eggs and buttermilk.
3. **Bread the Tomatoes:**
    - Dip each tomato slice into the flour mixture, coating both sides and shaking off the excess.
    - Next, dip the tomato slice into the egg mixture, allowing any excess to drip off.
    - Finally, coat the tomato slice again with the flour mixture, pressing gently to ensure a good coating.
4. **Heat the Oil:**
    - In a large skillet, pour enough vegetable oil to cover the bottom of the pan by about ½ inch. Heat the oil over medium-high heat until it reaches 350°F (175°C). You can test the oil temperature by dropping in a small piece of bread; it should sizzle and turn golden brown.
5. **Fry the Tomatoes:**
    - Carefully place a few tomato slices in the hot oil, being careful not to overcrowd the pan.
    - Fry the tomatoes for about 2-3 minutes per side, or until they are golden brown and crispy.

- Remove the fried tomatoes with a slotted spoon and transfer them to a plate lined with paper towels to drain any excess oil.
6. **Serve:**
    - Serve the fried green tomatoes hot, with your favorite dipping sauces, such as ranch dressing, remoulade, or a spicy aioli.

Tips:

- **For a Spicy Kick:** Add a pinch of cayenne pepper to the flour mixture.
- **For Extra Crispiness:** Let the breaded tomatoes rest on a rack for 10 minutes before frying to allow the coating to set.

Enjoy your Florida Fried Green Tomatoes as a delicious appetizer or side dish!

Cuban Pork Roast

Ingredients:

- **For the Marinade:**
    - 1 cup sour orange juice (or substitute with a mix of ½ cup orange juice and ½ cup lime juice)
    - 8 cloves garlic, minced
    - 1 tablespoon dried oregano
    - 1 tablespoon ground cumin
    - 1 tablespoon paprika
    - 1 tablespoon salt
    - 1 teaspoon black pepper
    - 1 teaspoon ground coriander
    - ¼ cup olive oil
    - 1 large onion, finely chopped
    - 1 tablespoon white vinegar
- **For the Pork Roast:**
    - 4-5 pounds pork shoulder (also known as pork butt or picnic roast), trimmed of excess fat

Instructions:

1. **Prepare the Marinade:**
    - In a bowl, combine the sour orange juice, minced garlic, dried oregano, ground cumin, paprika, salt, black pepper, ground coriander, olive oil, finely chopped onion, and white vinegar. Mix well to combine.
2. **Marinate the Pork:**
    - Place the pork shoulder in a large resealable plastic bag or a shallow dish.
    - Pour the marinade over the pork, ensuring it is well coated.
    - Seal the bag or cover the dish and refrigerate for at least 6 hours, preferably overnight, to allow the flavors to penetrate the meat.
3. **Preheat the Oven:**
    - Preheat your oven to 325°F (165°C).
4. **Roast the Pork:**
    - Remove the pork shoulder from the marinade, letting any excess marinade drip off. Discard the used marinade.
    - Place the pork shoulder on a rack in a roasting pan, or directly in the pan if you don't have a rack. You can also place it on a bed of sliced onions and garlic for extra flavor.
    - Roast the pork in the preheated oven for about 3-4 hours, or until the internal temperature reaches 190°F (88°C) and the meat is tender and easily shreds. The exact time will depend on the size of the roast.
5. **Finish the Roast:**

- For a crispy exterior, you can increase the oven temperature to 400°F (200°C) during the last 20-30 minutes of roasting. Keep an eye on it to avoid burning.
- Let the pork roast rest for about 15-20 minutes before slicing or shredding.

6. **Serve:**
    - Slice or shred the pork and serve it with traditional Cuban sides such as black beans and rice, fried plantains, or yuca with garlic sauce.

Tips:

- **For Extra Flavor:** You can inject some of the marinade into the pork shoulder before roasting for a deeper flavor.
- **For Crispy Skin:** If the roast has skin, you can score it before marinating and increase the roasting temperature towards the end to crisp it up.

Enjoy your Cuban Pork Roast with its rich, tangy flavors and juicy, tender meat!

Southern Pecan Pie

Ingredients:

- **For the Pie Crust:**
    - 1 ¼ cups all-purpose flour
    - ¼ cup granulated sugar
    - ½ teaspoon salt
    - ½ cup (1 stick) unsalted butter, chilled and cut into small pieces
    - 1 large egg yolk
    - 2-3 tablespoons ice water
- **For the Pecan Pie Filling:**
    - 1 cup light corn syrup
    - 1 cup packed brown sugar
    - ¼ cup unsalted butter, melted
    - 3 large eggs
    - 1 ½ teaspoons vanilla extract
    - 1 ½ cups pecan halves

Instructions:

1. **Prepare the Pie Crust:**
    - In a large bowl, whisk together the flour, granulated sugar, and salt.
    - Add the chilled butter pieces and use a pastry cutter or your fingers to work the butter into the flour mixture until it resembles coarse crumbs.
    - In a small bowl, whisk the egg yolk and 2 tablespoons of ice water together.
    - Gradually add the egg mixture to the flour mixture, stirring with a fork until the dough begins to come together. If the dough is too dry, add an additional tablespoon of ice water.
    - Turn the dough out onto a lightly floured surface and knead it a few times until it forms a cohesive ball.
    - Flatten the dough into a disk, wrap it in plastic wrap, and refrigerate for at least 30 minutes.
2. **Preheat the Oven:**
    - Preheat your oven to 350°F (175°C).
3. **Roll Out the Dough:**
    - On a lightly floured surface, roll out the chilled dough to fit a 9-inch pie dish. Transfer the dough to the pie dish and gently press it into the bottom and sides. Trim any excess dough and crimp the edges as desired.
    - Place the pie crust in the refrigerator while you prepare the filling.
4. **Prepare the Pecan Pie Filling:**
    - In a large bowl, whisk together the corn syrup, brown sugar, melted butter, eggs, and vanilla extract until well combined.
    - Stir in the pecan halves.

5. **Assemble and Bake the Pie:**
    - Pour the pecan pie filling into the prepared pie crust.
    - Bake in the preheated oven for 50-60 minutes, or until the filling is set and the top is golden brown. The center should be slightly jiggly but not liquid.
    - If the crust starts to get too dark before the filling is set, cover the edges with aluminum foil to prevent over-browning.
6. **Cool and Serve:**
    - Allow the pie to cool completely on a wire rack before slicing. This allows the filling to set properly.

Tips:

- **For a Crunchier Texture:** Toast the pecans lightly before adding them to the filling.
- **For a Smooth Filling:** Make sure to whisk the filling thoroughly to ensure a smooth, lump-free mixture.

Enjoy your Southern Pecan Pie, a sweet and nutty classic that's sure to please!

Key West Fish Tacos

Ingredients:

- **For the Fish:**
    - 1 pound white fish fillets (such as cod, tilapia, or snapper)
    - 1 cup all-purpose flour
    - ½ cup cornmeal
    - 1 teaspoon paprika
    - 1 teaspoon garlic powder
    - ½ teaspoon onion powder
    - ½ teaspoon salt
    - ½ teaspoon black pepper
    - 1 large egg
    - 1 cup buttermilk (or milk with 1 tablespoon lemon juice added)
    - Vegetable oil for frying
- **For the Slaw:**
    - 3 cups shredded cabbage (green or a mix of green and red)
    - 1 cup shredded carrots
    - ½ cup chopped fresh cilantro
    - ¼ cup mayonnaise
    - 2 tablespoons lime juice
    - 1 tablespoon honey
    - Salt and pepper to taste
- **For the Sauce:**
    - ½ cup sour cream
    - 2 tablespoons lime juice
    - 1 tablespoon chopped fresh cilantro
    - 1 teaspoon honey
    - ¼ teaspoon garlic powder
    - Salt and pepper to taste
- **For Assembly:**
    - 8 small tortillas (corn or flour)
    - Lime wedges for garnish
    - Fresh cilantro for garnish

Instructions:

1. **Prepare the Slaw:**
    - In a large bowl, combine the shredded cabbage, shredded carrots, and chopped cilantro.
    - In a small bowl, whisk together the mayonnaise, lime juice, honey, salt, and pepper.
    - Pour the dressing over the cabbage mixture and toss until well coated. Set aside.

2. **Prepare the Sauce:**
   - In a small bowl, mix together the sour cream, lime juice, chopped cilantro, honey, garlic powder, salt, and pepper. Adjust seasoning to taste. Set aside.
3. **Prepare the Fish:**
   - In a shallow dish, combine the flour, cornmeal, paprika, garlic powder, onion powder, salt, and black pepper.
   - In another shallow dish, whisk together the egg and buttermilk.
   - Dip each fish fillet into the egg mixture, allowing excess to drip off, then coat it with the flour mixture, pressing lightly to adhere.
   - Heat vegetable oil in a large skillet over medium-high heat. There should be enough oil to cover the bottom of the pan by about ¼ inch.
   - Fry the fish fillets for 3-4 minutes per side, or until golden brown and cooked through. Remove and drain on paper towels.
4. **Assemble the Tacos:**
   - Warm the tortillas in a dry skillet or on a griddle until pliable.
   - Break the fried fish into bite-sized pieces.
   - Spread a spoonful of the slaw onto each tortilla.
   - Top with pieces of fried fish.
   - Drizzle with the prepared sauce.
   - Garnish with lime wedges and additional fresh cilantro if desired.
5. **Serve:**
   - Serve the tacos immediately with extra lime wedges on the side for squeezing over.

Tips:

- **For a Spicy Kick:** Add a few dashes of hot sauce to the slaw or sauce.
- **For Extra Crispiness:** Let the coated fish rest for 10-15 minutes before frying to ensure a crisp coating.

Enjoy your Key West Fish Tacos with their fresh and vibrant flavors!

Florida Avocado Salad

Ingredients:

- **For the Salad:**
    - 2 ripe avocados, peeled, pitted, and diced
    - 1 cup cherry tomatoes, halved
    - 1 cucumber, peeled, seeded, and diced
    - ½ red onion, finely chopped
    - ¼ cup fresh cilantro, chopped
    - ¼ cup crumbled feta cheese (optional)
    - Salt and black pepper to taste
- **For the Dressing:**
    - 3 tablespoons extra-virgin olive oil
    - 2 tablespoons fresh lime juice (about 1 lime)
    - 1 teaspoon honey or agave syrup
    - 1 teaspoon Dijon mustard
    - 1 clove garlic, minced
    - ¼ teaspoon ground cumin
    - Salt and black pepper to taste

Instructions:

1. **Prepare the Dressing:**
    - In a small bowl, whisk together the olive oil, lime juice, honey or agave syrup, Dijon mustard, minced garlic, ground cumin, salt, and black pepper until well combined. Adjust seasoning to taste.
2. **Prepare the Salad Ingredients:**
    - In a large bowl, combine the diced avocados, cherry tomatoes, cucumber, red onion, and fresh cilantro.
    - Gently toss the ingredients together to combine.
3. **Add the Dressing:**
    - Pour the dressing over the salad and toss gently to coat all the ingredients evenly.
    - If using, sprinkle the crumbled feta cheese over the top of the salad.
4. **Season and Serve:**
    - Season the salad with additional salt and black pepper to taste.
    - Serve immediately, or chill in the refrigerator for up to an hour before serving.

Tips:

- **For Extra Flavor:** Add a pinch of red pepper flakes to the dressing for a bit of heat.
- **For Crunch:** Add some toasted nuts or seeds, like sunflower seeds or almonds, for extra texture.

- **To Prevent Browning:** If preparing the salad in advance, toss the avocado with a bit of extra lime juice to help prevent browning.

Enjoy your Florida Avocado Salad as a fresh and vibrant addition to your meal!

Spicy Conch Fritters

Ingredients:

- **For the Fritters:**
    - 1 pound conch meat, finely chopped (can be fresh or frozen; if using frozen, thaw and drain well)
    - 1 cup all-purpose flour
    - ¼ cup cornmeal
    - 1 teaspoon baking powder
    - ½ teaspoon baking soda
    - 1 teaspoon salt
    - ½ teaspoon black pepper
    - 1 teaspoon paprika
    - ½ teaspoon cayenne pepper (adjust to taste)
    - 1 teaspoon ground cumin
    - 1 small red bell pepper, finely chopped
    - 1 small onion, finely chopped
    - 2 cloves garlic, minced
    - 1 jalapeño pepper, seeded and finely chopped (optional, for extra heat)
    - 1 large egg
    - ½ cup milk (or buttermilk)
    - 2 tablespoons fresh parsley, chopped
    - Vegetable oil for frying
- **For the Dipping Sauce (optional):**
    - ½ cup mayonnaise
    - 2 tablespoons hot sauce
    - 1 tablespoon lime juice
    - 1 teaspoon honey
    - Salt and pepper to taste

Instructions:

1. **Prepare the Fritters:**
    - In a large bowl, combine the flour, cornmeal, baking powder, baking soda, salt, black pepper, paprika, cayenne pepper, and ground cumin. Mix well.
    - Add the chopped conch meat, red bell pepper, onion, garlic, jalapeño (if using), and fresh parsley to the dry ingredients. Stir to combine.
    - In a separate bowl, whisk together the egg and milk.
    - Pour the wet ingredients into the dry ingredients and mix until just combined. The batter should be thick and chunky.
2. **Heat the Oil:**

- In a large skillet or deep fryer, heat vegetable oil to 350°F (175°C). There should be enough oil to cover the bottom of the pan by about ½ inch. If using a deep fryer, follow the manufacturer's instructions for frying.
3. **Fry the Fritters:**
    - Using a spoon or small ice cream scoop, drop spoonfuls of batter into the hot oil.
    - Fry the fritters in batches, being careful not to overcrowd the pan. Cook for about 2-3 minutes per side, or until golden brown and cooked through.
    - Remove the fritters with a slotted spoon and transfer them to a plate lined with paper towels to drain any excess oil.
4. **Prepare the Dipping Sauce (optional):**
    - In a small bowl, whisk together the mayonnaise, hot sauce, lime juice, honey, salt, and pepper until well combined.
5. **Serve:**
    - Serve the spicy conch fritters hot with the dipping sauce on the side, if desired.

Tips:

- **For Extra Flavor:** Add a bit of chopped fresh cilantro to the batter for a burst of freshness.
- **For a Crispy Texture:** Ensure the oil is hot enough before adding the fritters, and avoid overcrowding the pan to maintain a crispy exterior.

Enjoy your Spicy Conch Fritters with their delicious blend of flavors and satisfying crunch!

Florida Lime Chicken

Ingredients:

- **For the Marinade:**
    - ¼ cup fresh lime juice (about 2 limes)
    - 2 tablespoons olive oil
    - 2 tablespoons honey or agave syrup
    - 3 cloves garlic, minced
    - 1 tablespoon soy sauce
    - 1 teaspoon ground cumin
    - 1 teaspoon dried oregano
    - 1 teaspoon paprika
    - ½ teaspoon chili powder
    - Salt and black pepper to taste
- **For the Chicken:**
    - 4 boneless, skinless chicken breasts or thighs (about 1 ½ pounds)
    - Lime wedges and fresh cilantro for garnish (optional)

Instructions:

1. **Prepare the Marinade:**
    - In a bowl, whisk together the lime juice, olive oil, honey, minced garlic, soy sauce, ground cumin, dried oregano, paprika, chili powder, salt, and black pepper until well combined.
2. **Marinate the Chicken:**
    - Place the chicken breasts or thighs in a large resealable plastic bag or a shallow dish.
    - Pour the marinade over the chicken, ensuring each piece is well coated.
    - Seal the bag or cover the dish and refrigerate for at least 1 hour, preferably 2-4 hours for maximum flavor. If marinating overnight, keep in mind the chicken might become very tangy.
3. **Cook the Chicken:**
    - **Grilling Method:**
        - Preheat your grill to medium-high heat.
        - Remove the chicken from the marinade and discard the excess marinade.
        - Grill the chicken for 6-8 minutes per side, or until the internal temperature reaches 165°F (74°C) and the juices run clear.
    - **Baking Method:**
        - Preheat your oven to 375°F (190°C).
        - Remove the chicken from the marinade and discard the excess marinade.
        - Place the chicken on a baking sheet lined with parchment paper or lightly greased.

- Bake for 25-30 minutes, or until the internal temperature reaches 165°F (74°C) and the chicken is cooked through. Optionally, you can broil the chicken for a few minutes at the end to get a slightly charred exterior.

4. **Serve:**
    - Let the chicken rest for a few minutes before slicing.
    - Garnish with lime wedges and fresh cilantro, if desired.

Tips:

- **For Extra Flavor:** Add a bit of lime zest to the marinade for an extra punch of citrus.
- **For a Spicy Kick:** Include a diced jalapeño or a pinch of red pepper flakes in the marinade.

Enjoy your Florida Lime Chicken with its bright and refreshing flavors, perfect for a light and satisfying meal!

Cuban Beef Empanadas

Ingredients:

- **For the Filling:**
    - 1 pound ground beef
    - 1 tablespoon olive oil
    - 1 small onion, finely chopped
    - 1 bell pepper, finely chopped (red or green)
    - 3 cloves garlic, minced
    - 1 teaspoon ground cumin
    - 1 teaspoon paprika
    - ½ teaspoon dried oregano
    - ½ teaspoon ground black pepper
    - 1 teaspoon salt
    - ¼ cup tomato sauce
    - ¼ cup green olives, sliced (pitted)
    - ¼ cup raisins (optional, for a touch of sweetness)
    - 1 large egg, beaten (for egg wash)
- **For the Dough:**
    - 2 ½ cups all-purpose flour
    - 1 teaspoon salt
    - ½ cup unsalted butter, cold and cut into small pieces
    - 1 large egg
    - 1/3 cup cold water (more if needed)

Instructions:

1. **Prepare the Filling:**
    - Heat the olive oil in a large skillet over medium heat.
    - Add the chopped onion and bell pepper. Cook until softened, about 5 minutes.
    - Add the minced garlic and cook for another minute.
    - Add the ground beef to the skillet and cook, breaking it up with a spoon, until browned and cooked through.
    - Stir in the ground cumin, paprika, dried oregano, black pepper, and salt. Mix well.
    - Add the tomato sauce and stir to combine. Let the mixture simmer for about 5 minutes.
    - Stir in the sliced olives and raisins (if using). Adjust seasoning if needed.
    - Remove from heat and let the filling cool slightly.
2. **Prepare the Dough:**
    - In a large bowl, combine the flour and salt.
    - Cut in the cold butter using a pastry cutter or your fingers until the mixture resembles coarse crumbs.
    - In a small bowl, whisk together the egg and cold water.

- Gradually add the egg mixture to the flour mixture, stirring until the dough begins to come together. Add more water if necessary, one tablespoon at a time.
- Turn the dough out onto a lightly floured surface and knead gently until smooth.
- Divide the dough into two portions, flatten each into a disk, and wrap in plastic wrap. Chill in the refrigerator for at least 30 minutes.

3. **Assemble the Empanadas:**
    - Preheat your oven to 375°F (190°C) and line a baking sheet with parchment paper.
    - On a lightly floured surface, roll out one disk of dough to about ¼-inch thickness.
    - Using a round cutter (about 3-4 inches in diameter), cut out circles of dough.
    - Place a spoonful of the beef filling in the center of each dough circle.
    - Fold the dough over the filling to create a half-moon shape. Press the edges together and crimp with a fork to seal.
    - Place the empanadas on the prepared baking sheet.
    - Brush the tops with the beaten egg for a golden finish.

4. **Bake the Empanadas:**
    - Bake in the preheated oven for 20-25 minutes, or until the empanadas are golden brown and crisp.
    - Remove from the oven and let cool slightly before serving.

Tips:

- **For Extra Flavor:** You can add a bit of chopped fresh cilantro or a dash of hot sauce to the filling.
- **For a Crispy Texture:** Ensure the dough is cold when rolling out, and avoid overworking it to keep it flaky.

Enjoy your Cuban Beef Empanadas with their savory, spiced filling and crisp, flaky crust!

Tropical Fruit Smoothie

Ingredients:

- **For the Smoothie:**
    - 1 cup frozen mango chunks
    - 1 cup frozen pineapple chunks
    - 1 banana, peeled and sliced
    - 1 cup coconut milk (or any milk of your choice)
    - ½ cup Greek yogurt (plain or vanilla)
    - 1 tablespoon honey or agave syrup (adjust to taste)
    - Juice of 1 lime (optional, for a tangy twist)
    - Ice cubes (optional, for a thicker texture)
- **For Garnish (optional):**
    - Fresh mint leaves
    - Sliced fruit (e.g., kiwi, strawberries, or pineapple)
    - Chia seeds or shredded coconut

Instructions:

1. **Blend the Ingredients:**
    - In a blender, combine the frozen mango chunks, frozen pineapple chunks, banana slices, coconut milk, Greek yogurt, honey or agave syrup, and lime juice (if using).
    - Blend on high speed until smooth and creamy. If the smoothie is too thick, add a bit more coconut milk or a splash of water. If it's too thin, add a few ice cubes and blend again.
2. **Adjust the Sweetness:**
    - Taste the smoothie and adjust the sweetness as needed by adding more honey or agave syrup.
3. **Serve:**
    - Pour the smoothie into glasses.
    - Garnish with fresh mint leaves, sliced fruit, chia seeds, or shredded coconut if desired.
4. **Enjoy:**
    - Serve immediately for the best flavor and texture.

Tips:

- **For Extra Creaminess:** Use full-fat Greek yogurt or add a small amount of avocado to the smoothie.
- **For a Protein Boost:** Add a scoop of protein powder or a tablespoon of nut butter.
- **For a Cooler Drink:** Keep the fruit frozen for a thicker and colder smoothie, or add a handful of ice cubes if using fresh fruit.

Enjoy your Tropical Fruit Smoothie, packed with tropical flavors and a touch of sweetness!

Florida Peach Cobbler

Ingredients:

- **For the Filling:**
    - 6 cups fresh peaches, peeled, pitted, and sliced (or 2 cans of peach slices, drained)
    - 1 cup granulated sugar
    - 1 tablespoon lemon juice
    - 1 teaspoon ground cinnamon
    - ¼ teaspoon ground nutmeg
    - 2 tablespoons all-purpose flour (to thicken)
    - 1 teaspoon vanilla extract
- **For the Topping:**
    - 1 ½ cups all-purpose flour
    - ½ cup granulated sugar
    - 1 tablespoon baking powder
    - ½ teaspoon salt
    - ¼ cup unsalted butter, cold and cut into small pieces
    - ¾ cup milk (whole milk or buttermilk)
    - 1 teaspoon vanilla extract
- **For the Garnish (optional):**
    - 1 tablespoon granulated sugar
    - ½ teaspoon ground cinnamon

Instructions:

1. **Prepare the Filling:**
    - Preheat your oven to 375°F (190°C).
    - In a large bowl, combine the sliced peaches, sugar, lemon juice, ground cinnamon, ground nutmeg, flour, and vanilla extract. Mix well until the peaches are evenly coated.
    - Transfer the peach mixture to a greased 9x13-inch baking dish or a similar-sized ovenproof dish.
2. **Prepare the Topping:**
    - In a medium bowl, whisk together the flour, sugar, baking powder, and salt.
    - Cut in the cold butter using a pastry cutter or your fingers until the mixture resembles coarse crumbs.
    - Add the milk and vanilla extract to the flour mixture, stirring just until combined. The batter will be somewhat lumpy.
3. **Assemble the Cobbler:**
    - Spoon the topping over the peach filling in dollops. It doesn't need to cover the peaches completely; the topping will spread and rise during baking.

    - If desired, mix together the additional granulated sugar and ground cinnamon, and sprinkle over the topping for added sweetness and flavor.
4. **Bake the Cobbler:**
    - Bake in the preheated oven for 40-45 minutes, or until the topping is golden brown and the peach filling is bubbling.
5. **Serve:**
    - Allow the cobbler to cool slightly before serving. It's delicious served warm, either on its own or with a scoop of vanilla ice cream or a dollop of whipped cream.

Tips:

- **For Extra Flavor:** Add a pinch of ground cloves or a splash of almond extract to the peach filling.
- **For a Crispier Topping:** Bake the cobbler on a lower rack in the oven to ensure the topping gets a nice golden color and crispy texture.

Enjoy your Florida Peach Cobbler, a delightful and classic dessert that's perfect for summer or any time you crave a comforting treat!